Wait 'till I tell you

Sally a Smith
nei
Sally a Crowne
30·11-03·

'mostly in boats'

Wait 'till I tell you

An Ulster boyhood, 1904 – 1914

Harry Cronne

THE
MINT
PRESS

First published in Great Britain by The Mint Press, 2003

ISBN 1-903356-33-4

Cataloguing in Publication Data
CIP record for this title is available from the British Library

The Mint Press
18 The Mint
Exeter, Devon
England EX4 3BL

Typeset in 10/14 Garamond 3
Page design by Topics – The Creative Partnership, Exeter
Cover design by Delphine Jones
Printed and bound in Great Britain by Short Run Press Ltd, Exeter

Contents

Dedicated
to the memory of
Theo Moody,
the distinguished Irish historian
who worked for peace,
understanding and reconciliation

Foreword

*T*hese memoirs of a child's life in Northern Ireland at the beginning of the twentieth century were written and illustrated by my husband, Professor Harry Cronne, many years ago, while recovering from a massive stroke which left his left side completely paralysed. They recall the earliest years of a very happy childhood spent at Katesbridge near the beautiful Mourne Mountains, and later by the wild waters of Strangford Lough, at Portaferry, at a time when Ireland was still undivided and the countries of Europe not yet embroiled in war.

Harry's father was a Presbyterian Minister, first to the Congregation at Katesbridge and then to that at Portaferry. Here with the sea only a few feet from the door of the manse, and a sailing boat of his own from very early years, Harry spent the formative years of his youth, and loved it with a passion he never lost. He does not write with emotional nostalgia about these years, but with keen observation, a kindly wit, and accurate recollection, characteristics also reflected in his drawings of the people and scenes around him.

He had, even before his schooldays, a very forthright and fearless approach to life, and on one occasion being compelled to listen to a more than usually long and erudite sermon by his father, looked straight at the pulpit and called out loudly in face of the whole congregation, `Stop talking Daddy, and come down from there'.

The memories of a child who could do that with no fear of the possible consequences are likely to be more than usually interesting.

L. M. Cronne
CHELDON
SEPTEMBER 2003

I

ARCADIA

*I*n the middle of the nineteenth century, somewhere in the outbacks of Ulster, two Presbyterian elders were bringing the minister his quarter's stipend. On the way they had earnestly discussed the finances of their church. As they approached the Manse, one said to the other: 'Aye, Willie John, there it is. Thirteen guid pun' and 'I declare tae God I dinna ken what he does wi' it – unless he gambles it! 'This anecdote was told by Alex Mawhinney to a very appreciative audience in my father's study, in the 1920s.

Alex was highly respected locally, the chemist in fact, to whom we always referred as 'The Apothecary', with its sly, but appropriate, suggestion of a character of Sir Walter Scott's. His appearance was in no way extraordinary, so all the more difficult to describe, as is his manner. The smooth, creamy, oval face, placid and demure, and the secretly merry eyes suggested to my irreverent mind that, somewhere far back in his ancestry, there was a Confucian sage or a Kai Lung, who saw the joke in the human predicament, as did Alex himself. The purring voice, honeyed it may have been by his own choicest linctus, combined with his throw-away style of narration and his quirkish parentheses, gave an exquisitely droll piquancy to his stories, which cold print cannot convey. The chance recollection of the anecdote, the narrator and the congruent setting all brought back a multitude of memories, inconsequent as dreams, but susceptible of order. I must follow the eminently sound advice given by the King in *Alice in Wonderland*: 'Begin at the beginning' said the King, gravely, 'and go on till you come to the end: then stop'.

In its Red Hand, Ulster, most famous of the provinces of old Erin, has a fitting symbol. The warlike, bloodstained past is ever present in innumerable manifestations, from the Cattle Raid of Cooley to the activities of the IRA.

Martial figures have trodden its soil: Cuchúllain and John de Courcy, Eoghain Ruadh O Neill and Somhairle Buidhe McDonnell[1], the Reverend William Steel Dickson and 'Galloper' Smith (better known as F E, Lord Birkenhead), 'Monty' and, if not Alexander of Macedon himself, certainly Alexander of Caledon, Templer and Rory O Brády. There were also the Craebh Ruadh, Red Branch Warriors, a crew famous in story, and the South Down Militia, famous in song as the terror of the land. I am not sure whether it was in this regiment, or in its southern opposite number, the Cork Militia, that the drill sergeants guided the first marching steps of recruits by requiring each to wear a twist of hay round the left ankle and a twist of straw round the right. So they drilled them: Hayfoot! Strawfoot! Hayfoot! Break up them sprachlin[2] camels! Hay! Straw! Hay! Straw! Hay! … Hay! … Hay! …

In what was eventually to become the County Down, a few miles upstream from where the town of Banbridge now stands, one of the early Anglo-Norman or Welsh-Norman invaders of Ulster, I suppose, had built a typical motte-and-bailey castle, a stockaded mound and enclosure, beneath the hill of Shanaghan. This was clearly intended to guard an important crossing place on the Upper Bann and routes along its valley from the Gap of the North and the wild country of Mourne, then inhabited, no doubt, by people who nourished strongly Normanophobic feelings. The site was admirably chosen, on a rise above the north-east bank, just where the river makes a big westward sweep. The modern name of the place is Katesbridge. I do not know who Kate was or how she came to be thus obscurely immortalised. I have a faint recollection of having heard that it occurred when the railway was being constructed, a generation or so before my birth.

The Motte, which we called simply the Mound, commands one of the loveliest views in a lovely county, and when it was built, it must have been a splendidly dominant military post. From the summit, which presumably had a wooden tower, the route could have been devastatingly enfiladed that is now carried across the Bann on one of those austere, stone bridges with gracefully springing arches that romantically enhance so many of Ireland's river scenes.

[1] *Pronounced Owen Roe and Sorley Boy (red Owen and yellow Samuel).*
[2] *Scrambling or moving clumsily.*

Katesbridge Smithy, about 1910. Morgan, the smith (3rd from left) and his son (right).

The earthen stockaded banks of the bailey enclosure must have crowned the steep slope up from the small stream or backwater to the south. On the east side a little brook would have been an obstacle to attackers, well within the most effective range of the garrison's archery. Beyond the backwater a big flat meadow is islanded between it and the main river.

Sites that are of military importance, because of the lines of communication they control, are often important also for economic, administrative, ecclesiastical and social purposes, for precisely the same reason. So a much later generation of strategists, liable to be faced at times by conditions not entirely dissimilar from those that influenced the castle builders, located there a small barracks for the splendid old Royal Irish Constabulary, which then constituted the 'polis'. Similarly, a Post Office official, who is unlikely to have been Anthony Trollope, chose an adjacent situation for a local office. Economic determinists might consider that their views are vindicated in the area. It is likely enough that there was a water-mill hereabouts in Norman times, if not earlier. Be that as it may, there was a scutch-mill, in the early years of the twentieth century and before, for the production of tow from flax grown locally, and possibly imported too, for I believe its owner was a flax-buyer.

Adjacent to the mill was a terraced row of sturdily built houses for the mill workers and others. My memory of these is insufficiently clear, and my knowledge of the vernacular architecture of the Ulster countryside much too inadequate, for me to attempt to date this little centre of rural industry. One thing, however, remains perfectly clear: the housing was, by present-day standards, deplorable in many ways, but the stone construction was much more substantial than that of most modern council housing. Nobody bothered very much about the deficiencies and the sometimes insanitary conditions, for accepted standards at the beginning of the twentieth century were very different from ours, even among the relatively well-off.

The presbyters of the area, no less wide awake to strategic considerations than the other parties, had chosen the very motte-and-bailey itself as the site for a church and its manse – ein feste Burg, surely! Here, then, with the addition of the still vitally important smithy down by the bridge, and a national school, a few houses and a railway station half-a-mile away beyond the river, was the hamlet that I knew in my earliest years.

The Manse was planted foursquare in the middle of the bailey which, with the slopes below it, formed a charming garden. The motte was encircled on top by a number of larches, and their trunks could be surrounded by a canvas screen, faintly reminiscent of the original stockade. It stands between the Manse and the church. With its superb view up the Vale of Bann to the Mountains of Mourne, it was an ideal place for sitting out on fine days and for afternoon tea, with all the formality of lace or embroidered cloth, silver and porcelain employed in the ritual in the spacious days of King Edward VII. The modern mug and platter would have been shocking.

Years later, when I had come to know something of the too frequently disedifying history of the Christian churches, that little church beside the Mound symbolised for me the Kirk and the austere, harsh, oppressive but not ignoble system of John Calvin, John Knox and their followers. The building was utterly plain, rectangular, rendered, with tall, oblong windows of clear glass. Within, it was similarly unadorned, with box pews of pitch pine and with oil lamps on tall standards along its two aisles. The pulpit, high, broad and bowed in the middle between straight wings, had a decidedly Jacobean appearance by reason of its dark balusters and the decent red velvet cushion upon which the great Bible rested. I can hear the note of the precentor's pitch-pipe, for there was no 'kist o' whistles' there then; how I laughed to see him take it from his waistcoat pocket and sound off 'poo-oop', like Mr Toad, before the choir and congregation burst into psalmody. I can see about me the faces of a peasantry grown hard in the struggle to live, and I can hear the deep roll of their voices as they sing, a little ironically, it might seem, in those surroundings:

> *How lovely is Thy dwelling place,*
> *Oh Lord of Hosts, to me;*
> *The tabernacles of thy grace*
> *How pleasant, Lord, they be.*

I can sense, in that clear memory, the marching feet of those who would 'take the kingdom of Heaven by storm', and feel the strong force of the Calvinist tradition. The lovely prose of the Psalms in the Anglican rite has never held for me the poignance of the Scottish metrical version, doggerel though so much of it is. The old psalm tunes, heard in memory's ear, can still bring tears to my eyes, like the terns' cries in early summer and the voices of the wildfowl on a winter estuary.

In that Arcadian spot I was born in October 1904, son of the Presbyterian minister of the time, in a world that now seems as remote as the empire of Montezuma and almost as fabulous. Just as, long ago, old people used to recall nostalgically the lost scent of musk, so I recall the peculiar sweetness of that rosy Edwardian sunset, which we are now taught to see as embodying the sinister quality of a red sky - or a red hand - in the morning. It was a sweetness

'at first ...'

that is, perhaps, characteristic of an old society on the brink of dissolution or of revolutionary change. A small Irish boy, even in a sheltered and happy home, in the early years of the twentieth century, could not for long retain his English contemporaries' false sense of a world at peace and utterly secure. By the beginning of the century's second decade – marked nearly enough, it so happened by Halley's portentous comet, which I saw from the Mound – I believe I sensed, uncomprehendingly and so without apprehension, the imminence of storm.

Whatever else may be said about the beginning of the twentieth century, it was universally agreed by its intellectuals, popular preachers (of whom there were many, clerical and lay), politicians and journalists that it was ushering in an age of unexampled opportunity. That was true, far beyond their wildest imaginings, but opinions then differed as to the forms it would take. On my nursery wall there hung a picture of a flying hansom cab, powered by a miscellaneous collection of small rotors, on the principle of the helicopter. The cabbie was speaking through the trap in the roof, to a terrified old gentleman on the passenger seat. Below could be seen some of the famous buildings of London from Tower Bridge to Westminster Abbey. It was entitled 'Where Shall I Drop You?' In various ways that picture was symptomatic of the time, not least in the sense that the grim realities were still mercifully concealed from us.

In my earliest and most vivid memory, at the age of perhaps less than

The author aged two

14

two, I had seized an opportunity that had presented itself to me and had run headlong from the kitchen into the summer. There is the stale smell in my nostrils of the 'boortree', or elder, by the gate of the drive, the resinous smell of cupressus along its sweeping curve and the heavy, cloying smell of mown grass. Butterflies flitter above the strawberry beds on the sunny banks below the terrace with its trim ranks of roses and calceolarias. There is the faint susurrus of the summer breeze in the poplars along the foot of the garden, the drone of insects, the squeak of hawking house-martens, the ventriloquial 'choc' of a coot in the reeds and the soothing, liquid monotony of the weir. Somewhere there is the chattering whirr of a horse-drawn grass cutter, but, above all other sounds, one rises insistently, the voice of the corncrake, harsh and unceasing, which with its crescendo and diminuendo, filled all the summer days and nights of my childhood.

Beyond the garden are meadows, lined with alder and aspen and willow, along a reach of the Upper Bann as clear as a chalk stream. Whin-fleeced drumlin hills roll away to where the blue Mountains of Mourne fill the southern horizon. I swerve aside from the path leading down through a wicket-gate to the backwater, where the old green-and-white boat lies, infinitely alluring, for there is the haunt of the fearsome 'Wiggleflop' and the horrifying 'Jamjack', which had been invented to discourage my investigations in that direction. I race, panting now, towards the front door and there, close to the drawing-room windows, pull up my pinafore-protected frock – for little boys were not then breeched so early as they and their sisters are now – and triumphantly relieve myself. Bubbling with laughter, I submit to the pursuing authority that had been so joyously defied. That episode marks the first independent, and certainly the most uninhibited, public appearance of the only British or Irish professor of Medieval history ever, to the best of my knowledge, born so entirely appropriately in a Norman motte-and-bailey castle.

II

JIMMY

For over six years at the beginning of the twentieth century, the time-eroded motte-and bailey castle that I have described was my home and the centre of my little world. I was born in an undivided Ireland, where there was no need to differentiate oneself as an Ulsterman. I claim no kinship with any of the clans or saints of my native land. Pups whelped in the stable do not rate as horses, but they have their uses, as any sporting Irishman would agree. My people on both sides are Gall in the land of Gael. Equally foreign, let me point out, are the ancestors of every Irishman who cannot trace his line beyond such pre-historic peoples as the *Milesians* and *Tuatha De Donann* or people of the Goddess Donu, to the aboriginal, pot-bellied *Firbolgs*. I was always given to understand that the second 'n' in our name was due to my great-grandfather, who had a rapscallion namesake whose cheques bounced, and he neatly dissociated himself in this way. I daresay he also thought that this gave the name a prestigious, though spurious, Huguenot appearance; in fact he had hit upon a characteristically Baltic one!

My father, James Kennedy Cronne, came of an old burgess family, a class stupidly denigrated nowadays. Probably, on balance of ill against good and remembering that the road to hell is paved with good intentions, it has done more for the human race than any other class. My knowledge of the family is based upon family traditions rather than accurate genealogical facts, for I never followed these up with older relatives, as I ought to have done, or by research, which I was well qualified to do. Other things always seemed more important. My people seem to have been Herefordshire yeomen in the sixteenth century, whatever their earlier situation, and by the early seventeenth century some of them were freemen of the London Vintners Company. Family tradition brings

16

us to Ireland with Cromwell, which is as much as to say under a curse; but people are vague about dates, and I think that, as Free Vintners, my forebears were more likely to have come at the time of the Plantation, which is just as bad. Nonetheless the Anglo-Irish were no mean race.

I do not know how long they pursued the even tenor of a Puritan life, but cheerfulness must early have broken in. There was no trace of Holy Willie in any of the older relatives I knew or of whom I heard tell, although they maintained the formal practice of their nonconformist religion. My grandfather and namesake was said to be happiest as a raconteur, smoking a cigar as he warmed his 'coat-tails' in good Victorian fashion. He managed linen mills, while his brother John, of an inventive turn of mind, invented a machine for spoke-stitching, whatever that may be. The expertise in linen of my uncle Thomas took him to the Russia of the Tzars and subsequently to the United States. He lost touch, and I only knew about him because of 'Tommy's Russian Box'. I am not sure whether this was supposed to be a tea-caddy or a cigar-box. It was curiously and intricately carved, and was the home of a locust (symbolic?) until this, together with the box, disintegrated in the 1940s.

The family was musical. My great-grandfather, the 'n-putter', was said to have perfect pitch. The men of subsequent generations had good voices too and were richly endowed with the gift of the gab – and the women also – without benefit of the Blarney Stone. They were, with the exception of my father, capable of bargaining like the meanest oriental huckster, in fractions of a penny, as behoved people engaged in the linen trade. A fraction of a penny more, or less, in the yard added up considerably in the hundred pieces, at least in those days of the golden sovereign. They would give their gains, and more, with a heart-and-a-half, to the first pathetic appeal, as likely as not a thoroughly undeserving one, that was made to them. They tended, like Sir Winston Churchill, to treat money as a commodity, the function of which was to be spent.

It was always impressed upon me, from my earliest childhood, that it was far better to go without, if need be, than ever to buy anything cheap and shoddy; the best would do. I therefore find present day shopping extremely frustrating, since the best, as I had always understood the term, is seldom available, and the shoddy and meretricious so universally accepted. The implementation of the maxim quite often did mean going without in my childhood and later, but the principle is infinitely more difficult to maintain now, when one is rudely put off with the assertion that 's no call for it'.

Money can never have been exactly abundant in my father's house, but in retrospect, it seem to me that life, even in a minister's family, was remarkably comfortable during the decade before the First World War, in a way that it would never be again in my lifetime. We were particularly rich in the services of others. I was never conscious in those childhood days of belonging to any class, least of all to one engaged, so we have been told, in grinding the faces of the poor. On the contrary, I was acutely conscious of being myself deprived at times, on my mother's initiative, for the benefit of the poor. Once, at least, it was for the benefit of some child for whom she realised, at the last moment, that she had forgotten to buy a Christmas present. 'That new little engine of yours, Harry; you'll never miss' – but oh, I did, I did. Generosity was a virtue not so much inculcated as taken for granted.

My father cared not at all about money. Never in his life did he accept for himself a fee for any of the ministrations that traditionally earn one for a parson. Such a fee from the well-to-do was

Jimmy

18

promptly paid into church funds; from the poor it was tactfully returned as a christening gift for the infant, or a wedding present for the bride, or, by what means I do not know, to the bereaved. I think he was always particularly anxious that anything of this kind should be passed on to poor wives, who rarely had anything to call their own.

Jimmy was seldom aware of what he was eating, but the minutest flaw in silver, linen, cutlery or china inevitably attracted his interested scrutiny, to the chagrin of my mother who, contrary to all experience, hoped that he would not draw attention to it in the presence of guests, who were so often there. Completely oblivious, he would hold the object aloft, innocently enquiring 'what is this?' in the tone of one who had made a surprising ecological find.

My father was a very remarkable product of his generation and, one might add, of his family, many of whom had great charm, combined with a tendency not to make the most of their considerable talents. He could easily have achieved eminence in any worldly career, but profound religious belief led him, late, to follow the calling of a minister of the gospel. I had almost written the humble calling, but that would have given an entirely false impression. He was certainly not a humble man, which is not to say that he was arrogant, though he was justifiably conscious of intellectual superiority. His was the pride in his calling which impelled Pope Gregory the Great to designate himself 'The Servant of the Servants of God'. That it was a calling in the fullest sense of the word my father never doubted, and he lived up to his belief. His standards were beyond the reach of common men and as the years went on all of us who knew him understood that we were 'poor earthbound groundlings in the light of his candid flame'. The words were those of our friend, Professor J E Todd.

In my childish eyes Jimmy seemed immensely tall in his formal frock coat and glistening silk hat, but altogether more debonair when, in those Edwardian high summers, he wore the straw boater and the white, flowered waistcoat that some dandies affected. No Edwardian gentleman would have been considered correctly dressed, even in informal wear, without a waistcoat, although a mere blazer was acceptable with cricket or tennis kit. Jimmy was an inch or two shorter than his brothers, who all topped six feet, but he did not appear at all dwarfed in tall company. My wife Ann, herself tall, who only knew him in the last three years of his life, remembers him as a tall man. As I first remember him, he was in his late thirties, his brown hair already thinning and receding, but his ginger moustache luxuriant in the Edwardian fashion. His most striking features were a noble brow and deep-set grey eyes with a glance at once piercing and quizzical beneath hooded eyelids or, no less characteristically, with the dreamy, reflective look of the poet and philosopher he was.

My father was very susceptible to feminine charms and I think he appealed very much to women. He needed intensely the sympathetic support and utter devotion that he received from my mother. It is my guess that there had been a pretty auburn-haired girl in his early life. Certainly he treasured a drawing of one, which hung in his study. He referred, in more than one of his verses, to his hot heart, and a remarkable poem, composed while listening to a performance of Wagner's Siegfried Idyll, fully bears this out. He ends an amusing set of verses critical of women's clothing in the 1920s with this couplet:

> *I swear by all the stars above you*
> *I tell you this because I love you.*

For him my mother was 'the splendid comrade with the regal heart'. He dedicated the manuscript of his collected poems 'To one who makes life beautiful and sweet I bring this tribute of a loving mind'. 'Comrade', 'loving mind' – did the hot heart still belong to some lost love of long ago? I should doubt it, certainly at the time, near the end of his life, when he wrote that dedication, and I have no doubt that the loving mind was totally devoted to my mother.

His friendships were, with one exception, deep and lasting. In one case I thought him uncharacteristically lacking in Christian charity, but as a very young man I had not the hardihood to put this to him; it would have been too deeply wounding. I may say, in parenthesis, that he always expected me to speak my mind and never showed resentment, though I fear he may occasionally have felt it. An old friend of his, a genial little man with beaming spectacles, whom I very much liked, had a moral lapse and fell foul of the Law. My father never forgave him and denied him the comfort that he could so well have given. It is not for me to judge, for I never knew all the facts of the case. Forgery was the man's crime and, if he had made use of Jimmy's name for unlawful purposes, the breach of friendship is understandable. I only know that painful heart-searching led to the renunciation of the old friendship, and the man's name was never mentioned again.

Jimmy was a competent violinist and in the days of my early childhood the house used to be filled with his melody. It was also sometimes filled with the 'ruthful noise and ghastful' of a teenage spastic girl whom he taught. What my old friend Wilson McDonnell remembers him playing was 'The Wind that Shakes the Barley'. The house also echoed, but not at the same time, with the voices of village children singing, with my mother at the piano. Added to these were liable to be the lamentable ululations of the fox terrier, Nan, and her son Ranji (named after the famous cricketer H H Prince Ranjitsinhji). Jimmy, like many of his contemporaries, had a passion for Wagner

> *Wagner! Poet in tones! Painter in sounds!*
> *Weaver of chords! Wizard of mystic spells!*

Some traumatic experience it must have been, of which he never spoke, later impelled him to renounce his old, finely-grained fiddle, which hung silent, like the Harp of Tara, on his study wall for the last twenty-five years of his life. I have no ready explanation to offer. When age came upon him, he grieved, but still in verse, that he had neglected music and poetry, and he wrote of the Muse:

> *I look with dreamy eyes around my room*
> *I see the treasured books stand, row on row.*
> *And then, within, I hear the voice of doom!*
> *Was it for these you left her long ago?*
> *But it was not for mere book learning that he forsook the Muses.*

Jimmy knew his limitations. He was a competent violinist, no more. He wrote no outstandingly distinguished poetry, but some lovely lines, for they were melodic in the manner of his day. So, in a poem called 'Love's Roses', one quatrain in six seems to me to glow, as one rose glowed for him among more self-assertive blossoms:

Then let thy yellow petals glow;
Distil thy fragrance o'er my book,
And when I fail to see, I'll look
Straight into thy warm heart, and know.

Thus the truant lyrist, but other selves crowd and jostle: the metaphysicist, for
  example, and the amateur of the physical sciences:

But silence? Who has ever framed its laws?
What are they? Where their statement to be found?

The problem thus posed, the philosopher and the scientist continue a Socratic
dialogue throughout the sleepless hours of a summer night, but it is the mystic who
adds the coda:

. . . . .yet on that cosmic sea,
Beyond tomorrow and today and yesterday,
Without a chart, naked and alone, I steer
Along the line between the white stars and the red;
Along the abysm between the living and the dead
My frail barque furrows through the cosmic drift,
Out to the dawn and destiny of man.

I think the star metaphor derived not only from Astronomy, but from the flashing buoys marking the dredged channel eastwards out of Belfast Harbour. All the same, Jimmy was well abreast of advances in Astronomy, and if there were any current views about 'cosmic drift', he would have known all about them. To walk with him on a starry night was to hear a discourse of the planets and the constellations and all the host of the heavens, theories of the universe, poetic fancies and mathematical speculations far beyond my inadequately numerate comprehension.

Jimmy was an eager student of the latest scientific thought, and not in popularized versions. He preferred his information from the thinkers' own record, without any intermediary. He was sufficiently a mathematician to find in mathematics an enjoyable relaxation. He was enough of a classicist to find endless pleasure in the philosophers and especially the poets. Although he greatly preferred Greek to Latin, he plunged joyously into the medieval Latin lyrics, when the work of a fellow-countrywoman, Helen Waddell, whom he remembered as a girl at Magherally, near Katesbridge, brought them to his notice. The knowledge of Hebrew that his theological training had entailed was never allowed to accumulate dust. His sermons were prepared – not written, ever – with the Hebrew or Greek text beside him, and the Vulgate and translations in modern languages and his library around him. He obviously used every means in his power to discover, as a preliminary, the precise meaning of his chosen text and all its nuances. He read widely and deeply, not only in English literature, but in German, French, Italian and Spanish, and of the four his favourite was German. He was a critical peruser of new theological and philosophical works, and also of the *Spectator* and the old Manchester *Guardian* to keep abreast of current affairs.

In his middle years Jimmy equipped a small chemical laboratory in an attic room, to help a struggling under-graduate and a village schoolmaster. There was some ingenious do-it-yourself apparatus. I found there a rugby football (not mine) neatly attached by rubber tubing, at one end to a pair of bellows, and to a blowpipe at the other. Thus the basic principle of the bagpipes, improved, was brought to the service of chemistry.

It is clear that Jimmy considered all this varied knowledge the barest minimum for the practice of his calling. It was not to be presented, raw as it were, to his congregation, nor to be used to stun it with learned allusions and quotations. It provided the basis and background of his thought about Christian belief. For him there could be no conflict between knowledge and true religion. The tragedy of his life may have been that concentration upon the intellectual side of his calling meant the neglect of his beloved music and poetry, and that he realized too late that these might have led him more surely to the insight he so ardently desired. He preached with increasing emphasis the doctrine of a loving God.

My father's knowledge sometimes took very unexpected forms. Although he was incapable of shooting at any living creature, he had a somewhat expert knowledge of sporting guns. This was revealed to me when I was buying a gun, and he drew my attention to the grain (if I have remembered correctly) of the barrels of one, which did not meet with his approval. I was an ignorant young man, who did not know that gun-barrels had a grain. A gun, for him, was not simply an engine of destruction, but an instrument of precision in which fine craftsmanship and a genuinely aesthetic quality were reflected. Oddly enough, he professed complete ignorance of the methods of the historian, but his own handling of Biblical history was masterly. I remember listening enthralled (as I rarely did) to a sermon, in which he expounded the social, economic, cultural, political and religious background of the book of the prophet Jeremiah. Sadly, I was the only person in the audience capable of appreciating the brilliance of that *tour-de-force* by a born teacher, and as a young academic teacher myself, I was filled with envy.

Jimmy was, above all, an utterly devoted pastor. He possessed in an extraordinary degree, the gift of comforting those in distress. He referred, in a poem, to 'life's duties that make blood-drops start,' and I think the metaphor was true of his pastoral work, as he understood and performed it. His people's sorrows and joys were his own. Liking people and taking them, genially and uncondemningly, as he found them, they responded, even when his ideas and his way of expressing them seemed strange. His conversations often ended with a laugh, because he had hastily made a joke to give vent to the laughter he could no longer restrain, at some solemnly intended remark.

Revelling in dialect, as Ulstermen do more than most, and in private a good mimic, he habitually spoke and wrote the purist English. Not surprisingly, he was a notable talker and a compulsive teacher, and so his sermons were always far too long. New facets of his theme presenting themselves in his active mind, even as he preached, he forgot the few concise notes he had made on a tiny scrap of paper, not to mention wifely and filial exhortations, as he soared away, regardless of time. Many a good Sunday joint must have spoiled in consequence. It was said that, on my very first appearance in church, I called out: 'Stop talking, Daddy, and come down from there' – almost the selfsame words that Oliver Cromwell, under similar provocation, addressed to another preacher: 'Cease thy prating, Sir, and come down.'

Conversation was a different matter, one of give and take, for there were always people who enjoyed a good crack, or a cracking good discussion of any matter of moment. These my father invited home on Sunday evenings. They came to participate in lively talk, not to listen to any kind of set piece, such as many famous Irish talkers, like Mahaffy and Gogarty, indulged in, oddly convinced that they were conversing. For those it was a game, in which the conversational ball was to be captured and retained. Perhaps Jimmy was too tired, by that time, to talk at length, and he would certainly have punctured a selfish and conceited talker. Everyone who had a point of view, or a good story – that is everyone – had his say, and the wives sometimes did a neat piece of common-sensical puncturing when a spouse showed signs of getting out of hand.

Father was a very formidable champion of his people's rights, especially against high Bumbledom, however exalted. No lawyer could more effectively tear an opponent's arguments to pieces and hold them up to ridicule. He knew many influential people and sought their support unashamedly when an injustice had to be exposed and righted. He could hardly avoid being involved to some extent in politics; that would have been too much to expect in Ulster. He had scant respect for politicians as such, though I think he made an exception in favour of A J Balfour, who was by way of being a philosopher. In fact, he had friends among Ulster politicians on both sides. A set of verses about the general election of January, 1910, displays his contempt for the pettiness of churchmen in politics. It only alludes obliquely to some of the big issues of the time, which is surprising, but it is an amusing squib, and so it is printed in the Appendix.

His hot heart, as is the case with most of us, was liable to be carried away beyond his cooler judgement in a great crisis, but he had a very tender feeling for those of other persuasions, and sympathised deeply with them, while deploring all violence. Jimmy was intensely proud to be an Irishman, even if only a foster-son, and he was conscious of his country's need for freedom to fulfil her destiny. The destiny that he looked to for Ireland was highly idealistic and impractical, involving the rejection of the gross materialism that he attributed to England, and the cultivation, instead, of the Arts and the promotion of peace. His thoughts seemed indeed to run on the lines of the classical doctrine of Irish Nationalism, a magnanimous ideal, as propounded by Thomas Davis and the abortive Young Ireland Movement of the 1840s. In that spirit he was prepared to support the Liberal-Unionist cause, in so far as it was liberal, out of loyalty to his church and people, but in English terms he could never have been a Tory.

It is perhaps obvious that, as a boy, I did not find Jimmy an easy father. His standards were too high and he expected far too much of me academically, an unrealistic range of subjects, which he referred to as 'keeping ones options open.' When all this was sorted out in the Upper Fifth form, I found him a splendid and understanding friend.

Jimmy died in a lovely Maytime in 1937, in his seventieth year and on the point of retirement; died where he loved to be, as he had once written of Portaferry when on holiday in England:

> *But it all means nought to me,*
> *O'er the sea my thoughts are winging*
> *And I close my eyes and dream*
> *Of the woods, and bays, and barrows*
> *And the low road round the shore,*
> *For my heart sails in the narrows*
> *Between Killard Point and Bankmore.*
> *Like a lover nought estranges,*
> *In whatever scenes she be;*
> *So my heart, 'mid all the changes,*
> *Will forever turn to thee.*

III

BESSIE

*M*y mother's character was much less complex than my father's. She was Elizabeth Jane Sloane of Lisburn and came of Plantation stock. Her forebear, Alexander Sloane of Dunlop, Ayrshire, came to Ulster in the reign of James VI and I in the service of his kinsman and patron James Hamilton first Viscount Clandeboy, whose family's inordinate appetite for land and revenues won them the name of 'The Hungry Hamiltons'. I believe this was the view of their fellow Planters as well as of the Irish. Alexander became the Receiver of Taxes in Co. Down. He died in 1660, leaving, I think, seven sons. My mother was descended from the eldest of these, James, Barrister at Law, of the Inner Temple and MP for Thetford. He lies, or at least lay before the London blitz, in the Temple Church. The youngest of Alexander's sons was Hans, Baronet, of Chelsea, MD, PRS, PRCP. He succeeded Sir Isaac Newton as President of the Royal Society. His collection, bought for the nation, formed the basis of the British Museum. Two great-grandsons of Alexander, James of Loughgall, Co. Armagh, and Henry of The Diamond in the same county, my thrice great-grandfather, were prominent in the so-called 'Battle of the Diamond' in 1795 and in the founding, for good or ill, of the Orange Order.

Genial, jaunty little men the Sloanes were, at least those of an older generation than mine whom I knew. How typical were my distant Sloane cousins, who came over from Canada during the First World War, with their tight breeches, smart tunics, jingling spurs and gunners' swagger. Just so I imagined my maternal ancestors in seventeenth-century Ulster, for I doubt whether they would have been tall, like that born soldier and bonny fighter, my first cousin Harry.

Bessie was wont to announce, Cassandra-like, that the best of the summer was over once the twelfth of July was past. This was an eminently justifiable meteorological rather than politically inspired belief, like late snow lingering in the ditches, which she always said was 'waiting for more'. She had spent a good deal of time in her girlhood with her Scott cousins in Annaclare, Co. Armagh, and was well grounded there in good old fashioned country lore and equally good, old fashioned housekeeping. Her old fashioned blackberry cordial was a delight in the same degree that her springtime blood-purifying draught, based on flowers of sulphur, lemons and goodness only knows what else, was an abomination. Even worse for a small boy with a chesty cold, was to be rubbed not, like John Brown's baby, with camphorated oil, but with chilli paste. It was thus I learned to dance the Highland Fling!

My maternal grandfather, Henry Sloane of Lisburn, was agent for Sir William Wallace's property there and in Antrim. So, appropriately enough, a representative of a family which produced one of the great English collectors of the late seventeenth and early eighteenth centuries, entered the service of the founder of the Wallace Collection, who had inherited from the Marquess of Hertford, another notable collector.

Bessie, as I first remember her, was small and golden-haired, in a voluminous dress reaching to the ground, and with what I believe were called 'leg-of-mutton', or 'bagpipe', sleeves, which were baggy to the elbow and tight from there to the wrist, with many tiny buttons. For a toddler the skirts were useful to hang on to and to hide behind. Bessie was affectionate and gay in its true sense. For me and for other children she was also a disciplinarian who stood no nonsense. She had no intellectual pretensions whatsoever, but was well endowed with shrewd common-sense and a gift, as well as a liking, for organization. In short, she was one of those small women who get their own way. She was strongly religious, having been brought up in the low-church atmosphere of the Church of Ireland (as it has continued to be called in spite of disestablishment). She was more than a little inclined to innocent superstition, which she must have tried, not very successfully I am sure, to conceal from my father. My mother was most kind-hearted and generous. She loved her church work, especially with the young who, in those days, were amenable and did what they were bid – they better had! In that unsophisticated age and rural milieu she taught the village children to sing folk songs and Negro spirituals and Christmas carols. Music of the lighter kind was her delight and, before their marriages separated them, she and her sisters and brother Jim formed what might now be called a family pop group. Bessie was the pianist, Alice the violinist and Jim the banjoist. The banjo was the in-instrument then, as Kipling's 'plunka-hunka-hunka-hunka-hink' poem testifies. What the other two sisters played I do not know.

Above all, Bessie was hospitable in the extreme and she nourished deep family feeling – family, that is, in the extended sense, embracing cousins of all degrees and generations. During the Great War she took delight in entertaining whole batteries of Canadian cousins on leave, who shared her family feeling. All were entitled to her unwavering loyalty, her assistance if they needed it and her hospitality at all times. I found, after her death at the age of nearly 86, an astonishing international network of family correspondence, quite beyond my ability or desire to keep up.

It seems in retrospect, though my memory may exaggerate the numbers and telescope the occasions, that the house in Katesbridge was, more often than not, full of relatives and family friends, for Jimmy and Bessie were obviously a popular young couple. The occasional visiting cleric or missionary on furlough seemed to me intolerably stuffy (though some were in fact far from that) compared with my lively uncles, aunts and cousins, actual and 'bloodless'. I would include the Rev. Billy Morrow and the Rev. Mosey Logan among the far from stuffy clerics. Some missionaries on furlough from China registered strongly on my childish olfactory system, uncontaminated as it then was. The scent was indescribable, mysterious, not sweet but not unpleasant, perhaps like faded garlic flavoured with sandalwood, anchovies and Russian tobacco-smoke.

The Author and Mother, 1906.

29

Guests, 1906,
Robert Moffett, Isobel Moffett and Ranji, Jimmy, Janie Newton, Nan, Bessie.

There must have been long periods of *ennui* for a small boy, in those days long before radio and television, but I do not remember them. There was the endless fascination of the river, the boat and the fly-fishers, whom I was sometimes allowed to accompany, and the various doings of the countryside. There is always much more going on there than the inhabitants of towns ever realize. My mother taught me to read at a very early age and I cannot now recall being read to because I could not read for myself. There were lots of books in the house, but I must have early understood that the books in the study were not for me except for some volumes of exploration with fascinating illustrations. The travels of the Asiatic explorer Sven Hedin, in particular, captured my young imagination; I mean the illustrations rather than the text. My early reading, up to about the age of twelve, included Jane Austen, Scott, Dickens, *Robinson Crusoe* in a lovely old edition with quaint engravings, and others which few children nowadays would read at that age. I discovered for myself such light-hearted authors as Barry Pain, W W Jacobs and Jerome K Jerome. Robert Louis Stephenson, having delighted me with *Treasure Island, Kidnapped* and *Catriona,* turned me off with some of his other works. I also read the rival *King Solomon's Mines* by Rider Haggard, and there were the still popular R M Ballantyne 'the Brave' and G A Henty. Kipling delighted me more as a master of versification (which I tried to emulate) than as a storyteller. This kind of early free-range reading was no doubt beneficial and, having no faintest idea of judicious skipping, I ploughed right on through the whole of *Robinson Crusoe,* for example, moralisings and all. There were, however, some serious drawbacks. I early acquired an invincible dislike of Shakespeare's *Othello* and King John, and also a deeply rooted prejudice against Thomas Hardy, which I have never entirely overcome. Jude, who was the cause of it, not Tess, has remained impenetrably obscure ever since. Reading easily, too easily, at an early age, I did not have to spell words out. One result of this was almost incurably bad (phonetic) spelling.

All in all, my earliest memories are of music and much laughter, not at all, I daresay, the conventional idea of life in a Presbyterian manse in the early years of the twentieth century.

IV

ARCADIANS

When I was a tiny boy I was often taken out on a cushion tied to the bar of my father's bicycle, but both my parents were great walkers. I was soon provided with a donkey, Nellie, on which I accompanied them. I vividly remember riding home across the bridge from the railway station, on a brand-new saddle that had just arrived there. I am sure that the High King riding into Tara in his war chariot, with all the trumpets of Erin sounding (or perhaps it would have been harps?) could not have felt more proudly elevated than I did. Nellie was a temperamental creature, and she gave me a spectacular toss or two before I acquired a reasonably firm seat, except when passing a menacing steamroller. One toss occurred when she spied a basin which had contained chicken feed in a farmyard, and she made a bolt for it. The cuddie's fat belly presented difficulties for little legs, for she had a passion for bran mash, with sliced potatoes, to which my mother pandered shamelessly. The only way to capture Nellie on her island pasture was to entice her with the tin basin in which this delicacy was usually presented to her. Witch-like, she stubbornly refused to cross running water, so that the sides of the wooden bridge over the backwater had to be screened with hessian to prevent her seeing it.

There was one place on our peregrinations where I was rather afraid to go. A neat wicket-gate led through a high, shaggy hedge into an orchard. Within could be seen a painted soldier, whose arms whirled intermittently in the fitful breeze. By the gate was a notice which read 'STOP, TRESPADGERS PARSECUTED. Whoever does not stand when spok to shall receive shot'. I think that perhaps the text of the notice is pure family folklore, but the board was there.

Fishing

I particularly approved of one walk, which took us by a small, remote shop, whose proprietors were my friends Mr and Mrs Sam Potts, for there it was hoped that sweets might be bought. In church the old couple sat immediately behind the Manse pew. They composed themselves for the sermon with strong peppermints, and Mrs Potts, to my mother's annoyance, usually managed to slip one to me over the back of the pew. A very little boy, I then retired to a hassock on the floor, savouring my peppermint with long, delicious ice-cold breaths, to my poor mother's even greater annoyance.

I owed a good deal of my entertainment in those days to Minnie, a maid. She was a local girl, quite unsophisticated, who endeared herself to me by never treating me with the disapproval, or worse, the condescension that grownups so often displayed at a time when it was usual for children to be taught, very firmly, their place in the scheme of things. An exacting standard of behaviour was established for them, and there were difficult and futile maxims, such as that they should be seen but not heard. That, surely was an incitement to quiet mischief ('go and see what Master Harry is doing and tell him to stop') or to eavesdropping on adult conversation ('Mummie, *how* does Miss MacLintock set her cap at the new doctor? Sure she hasn't got one').

Dear Minnie, she had the instincts of a poacher, but no great skill on the practical side. Perhaps she failed to observe closely enough and to practice the methods of those versed in such fine arts. She made, at first, the grave tactical error of introducing the rabbit snare, which was heavily frowned upon, but she applied the principle of the noose in another way which, if observed, was not prohibited, but my idea of using my father's trout rod for it was. She attempted to catch the wild little brown trout, lying below the bridge over the backwater, by mounting a horsehair noose on a hazel or a withy wand and floating it downstream over them. Needless to say, she had no success in this infinitely delicate exercise.

I think it was Minnie, though possibly my mother, who pacified me by suggesting a roll of bacon as substitute for the live frog bait which, Isaac Walton notwithstanding, was vetoed. Highly successful that bacon was too, for my first, slightly intimidating, pike. Few trout of similar weight, and such have been few and far between, taken delicately on a carefully selected fly, ever gave me such unalloyed pleasure as that little two-and-a-half pound jack, caught (dare I admit it?) on a nightline. My father took me to it in the morning in the boat, propelling it, goodness knows why, with a long-handled shovel, such as roadmen used to use. I learned then that quenelles of pike can hold their own with dishes of daintier fish.

It was in Minnie's company that I was admitted to the freedom of the world of J M Synge, in a barn where a flail was still used to thresh out the odd sheaf of corn, and in a cow byre where girls milked by hand, squirting a sly jet at their bantering boyfriends lounging in the doorway. The talk and the laughter did not entirely register with me at that tender age, and I remember none of it. The vivid impression in my childish mind was of a happy, merry company, and so it was for the moment. I know well that those country lads and girls felt the pinch of poverty and the terror of disease. The great killer then was tuberculosis, called consumption. Diphtheria, scarlet fever and all the rest reaped their fearful annual quota, and even measles was a killer.

In spite of everything, on a country road after milking time on a May evening there was carefree merriment. A shock-headed rustic in a shapeless 'duncher' cap, coarse grey flannel shirt, collarless but with a brass stud in the neckband, mole-catcher's waistcoat unbuttoned, dusty, stained corduroy trousers strapped below the knee (to keep the rats out they told me) and great galumping boots carelessly laced, sat on a bank under a lilac hedge, coaxing a tune out of a little squeeze-box concertina. Boy and girl, hobnails and neater boots laced knee high, tapped their antiphonal rhythm on the dusty, untarred macadam, to the clapping, skelloching, laughter and banter of the onlookers. Had this been in England, Isaac Walton might have strolled up from the river, with his long angle-rod and a brace of fine trout, to ask for a syllabub to be stroked, or Samuel Pepys might have descended eager-eyed from his new coach,

'May Day Old Style'

to find as congenial company there as any described in the golden page of English literature. Ireland did not lack her own Waltons. Memories of such scenes still give me a sense of continuity with an older, happier world.

It is quite likely that a poke (a strip of paper twisted into a cone) of 'conversation lozenges' was passed round. I could not quite understand the proverbial objection to buying a pig in a poke. There were sweetie pigs and sweetie mice, both white and pink, with string tails, and such pigs were just as acceptable to me in a poke as in any more elegant package. Conversation lozenges were a form of social ice-breaker than which not even 'licker is quicker', as Ogden Nash claimed. About the size and thickness of today's ten-penny piece, but of various colours, geometric shapes and pungent flavours, including the favourite chlorodyne, they had Christmas-cracker kinds of sentiments printed on them in blotchy type. These ranged from the most banal remarks to the most daringly, for those times, amorous. There used to be a country saying that 'sure it's no use hissin' a man on til a weddin' he doesn't want', a situation to which injudicious use of the conversation lozenges would sometimes lead.

Two other personages, in addition to a Maggie I can scarcely recall, were on the strength at the Manse. James Bell McIlroy, father of Minnie, was the Sexton and odd-job-man. With his grizzled beard and weatherbeaten complexion, he seemed to me a very old man, almost a Biblical character, one of the workers in the vineyard. I had good cause to remember an occasion when, in the Vestry in my presence. He discovered some unconsumed communion wine. He swigged it with gusto, having given me an incriminating taste. Innocent child that I was, I mentioned this to my mother. My earnest endeavours to reduce the taste to pinhead proportions in no way served to save my bacon, or rather ham. No doubt this episode was the occasion for a sharp lesson to James Bell also.

I remember him as my instructor in the art of deracinating nettles with the bare hand. I was not an apt pupil for I did not believe him

> *Tender-handed stroke a nettle*
> *And it stings you for your pains;*
> *Grasp it like a man of mettle*
> *And it soft as silk remains.*

quoth James Bell. This was all very well in theory, but I was tender handed and not at all a man of metal, as I supposed it to mean. I did, with much hesitation, try it later on a very little, wee, baby one. The old boy was famous, at least in our family, for his sibylline sayings. 'As I often says tae Sam', he once remarked, 'if ye don't exceed, ye'll never process'. That was for long a catch-word with us. His classic description to my father of a visiting clergyman of small stature may, or may not, be fittingly recalled, but here it is: 'When he got up til praich he was buggered in two ways, for he c'uldny see ower the dask and he c'uldny get weel away wi' it.'

The other personage was Macgregor McIlroy, the gardener. He must have been quite a young man, though not in my eyes. He was immensely tall and gangling and he wore a full beard. Although his distant ancestor was, no doubt, a redhead, this beard was black as jet and would have done credit to the pirate Teach, known as Blackbeard, or to the prophet Moses. He was a gentle soul, who talked to me, as to nobody else, on easy terms, for out mental ages did not greatly differ. There was a special bond between us, established when in some dire emergency, and it must indeed have been dire, I was thrust into his arms to hold when I was a few weeks old. He was a special friend, who brought me little presents of apples or hazelnuts, or some hedgerow trifle, and eventually a tabby kitten called Fluff. I also had a black rabbit called Snowball and a white one called Smuts (for the Boer War was still a recent memory). Poor Macgregor was distressingly bashful, and when any stranger came into the garden where he was working, he would bolt for cover like a jackrabbit. At the time this seemed to me perfectly natural, for I might have done the same myself. No village concert would have been complete without his presence, for some funny man was sure to make a sly allusion to him, perhaps singing 'Macgregor from beside the Bann' instead of the legitimate line in the popular song 'Kelly from the Isle of Man'. This Kelly character had attributed to him by the local boys a number of physical peculiarities, such as a yellow belly and an iron hand. The merest pretence of an allusion to him sent Macgregor pitiably bolting for the nearest door or cover that was always inadequate, amid a storm of whistling, stamping and applause. Rustic hobnails and the 'wheeps' produced by inserting large fingers in big bucolic mouths made a stupendous din.

I must have been a lonely little boy, although I cannot now remember feeling so. Apart from the visits of cousins or friends, there were no children with whom I was allowed to play. I might converse, but only through the bars of the gates, with village children, who sometimes stopped to talk to the strange little chap who did not speak the vernacular. One of them sometimes played, between the bars, a splendid roll on my drum (a properly headed one) that would have gratified Sir Francis Drake.

The imposition of that quarantine by my parents was probably due partly to fear of my being led away into trouble, but it must have been mainly on grounds of hygiene. Infections and contagious diseases were rife. Some of the poorest children bore the most loathsome stigmata of under-nourishment and vitamin deficiency, dirt and disease. They had ringworm on their closely cropped heads with the long dusty-looking fringes over their foreheads, great scabs on their faces and around their mouths and sores on their legs, and, pretty certainly, vermin. There was one very common indisposition: 'Liza Jane has a bile on her bum an' it's bealin' (suppurating). Bealing, indeed, seemed rife beyond all the other ills that the flesh of rustic childhood was heir to. People were very fearful of tetanus, called lockjaw, and of any cut between thumb and forefinger, which was believed to be an ineluctable cause of it.

Toothache, or faceache, was very common, but little resort was had to dentistry, partly because people could not afford it, partly because of fear of the dentist's drill. Palliatives were sought in oil of cloves or whiskey, a tot of which at three-and-six a bottle would have cost few old pence; and there were ways of coming by poteen. It was only in sheer desperation that sufferers went to the doctor to have the offending tooth removed, for the doctor was available locally. The more difficult the extraction, the prouder they were, boasting that 'sure he could har'ly loose it'.

There was one unfortunate little girl whom some ghastly accident had left with mutilated stumps of hands. It was my duty, from time to time, to shake hands with her, which I suspect may have embarrassed her as much as my small, quailing self. My mother had a most tender feeling for all her fellow creatures, human and animal, but I do not suppose it ever occurred to her that her small son and the little girl might have different feelings.

Here and there on country roads I remember the old stone-breaker, who would probably have been a pensioner if the old age pension had yet existed. He wore wire-mesh goggles to protect his eyes, as he sat on a pile of large stones knapping away with his long-handled hammer. The road metal produced by this time-consuming, palaeolithic toil was worked in by a steam-roller on a main road, or on a by-road was spread deeply and left to be ground down by traffic in the course of time.

Besides native Arcadians there were transients. The Packman was a regular visitor, with his heavy pack slung on a broad strap. It contained materials of various kinds, articles of women's and children's clothing, ribbons, garters, needles and thread, hatpins and all other kinds of pins, men's watch-chains of cheap metal for the Sunday waistcoat-pocket, small toys and gew-gaws such as street hucksters used to sell. He was dressed in heavy, dark tweed, with an old fashioned billycock hat, and he carried a heavy, blackthorn stick. This, besides supporting him over the weary miles, was useful for dealing with fierce farm dogs and even as a weapon of defence, if need be. He remains in my mind a formidable figure.

There was the 'Delft Man', who itinerated in a spring-cart filled with crockery and china of all sorts. He offered lustre teapots, hot-water jugs of heavy glazed brown pot with counterbalanced lids, ornamental jugs of a rather Germanic type with scenes from Shakespeare's plays. I am not sure that one of these, showing Falstaff with a Merry Wife of Windsor, did not bear the legend *DURST BLEIBT IMMER*. There were also mugs and quantities of coarse cups decorated with an Ace of Clubs design.

There were two men who led a dancing bear on a fathom of chain. I particularly remember the scene at our kitchen door, when my mother, with 'Ah, the poor thing' insisted that the bear's muzzle should be removed, much against the wishes of the bear-wards, so that she could feed it an almost untouched section of honey in the comb. The bear-wards being suitably bribed, I beat a hasty retreat, but I have no doubt that the bear enjoyed an agreeably slurpy interval.

On almost any road, we were liable to see the incarnation of one of the symbols of Erin, the *Sean Bean Bocht*[3], or Poor Old Woman. There she sat beneath a hedge, huddled in her black shawl, puffing away at her short,

---

[3] *Usually spoken of as the Shan Van Vocht.*

WAIT 'TILL I TELL YOU

nosewarmer pipe. Perhaps she was crooning to herself of Deirdre of the Sorrows or Grania of the Golden Hair, but much more likely, she was just praying; as Padraic Colum wrote 'for a little house out of the wind's and the rain's way'. I do not remember any of them begging.

Retrospectively it is deeply saddening to reflect that, in Ireland at the beginning of the twentieth century, the appalling problems of unemployment, poverty, disease, hunger and inadequate housing took so poor a second place in the public concern to politics and the struggle for and against Home Rule. Old Age Pensions were established before we left Katesbridge in 1911, and there was a constant stream of applicants at the Manse for their 'baptism lines', in order to establish their claim to it. The Labourer's Cottage, a new type of small, compact house built to a standard pattern had also made its appearance by then. Things were beginning to improve, but much remained to be done, when critical developments in Ireland and England and on the Continent postponed further progress.

40

V

POWER

*T*he first thing to strike a modern eye about most of the country roads three-quarters of a century ago would be that, while they were macadamised, they were not tarred. In summer they were so dusty that the hedgerows were whitened as by the proximity of a cement works. In winter they were full of rain-filled potholes and a slurry of mud. The advent of the motorcar would soon change all that. The next thing to impress a modern observer would probably be the absence of traffic, especially fast traffic. There was an occasional farm cart, or a baker's van on its leisurely round, or a doctor's or prosperous farmer's dashing gig, or dogcart with its beautifully groomed, high-stepping mare, an occasional horseman, or a lady riding side-saddle, or even Harry Cronne on his donkey. Sometimes one saw a steam-roller, or a traction-engine towing a threshing-machine to a farm. In the evening, as likely as not, a village girl was being helped, or hindered, by an ardently supportive swain, as she strove to master the art of riding a 'safety bicycle'. A carriage was a rare sight in the deep countryside, for other, lighter vehicles were more practicable. One of the drawbacks of horse-drawn transport was that passengers in heavy, and even not so very heavy, vehicles, had to walk up the stiff hills, but this was also true of the early motorcars. Horses, at least, did not have to be backed uphill, as motorcars were sometimes obliged to be in the days of my early childhood.

A motorcar (not yet shortened to car) was so rare and exciting a thing on a country road that a child ran to see it pass or, even better, break down as it so often did. At this early stage, motorists seemed to make light of what would nowadays be considered major disasters, such as damage to the gearbox or a crack in the cooling system. Repairs seemed often to be within the competence of any blacksmith sufficiently 'bloody, bold and resolute' to tackle them. Such a man had his foot on the road to modest, or even great, fortune, if he launched out as an automobile engineer or a garage proprietor. After all, William Morris began with bicycles.

There was always ample notification of a motorcar's approach, which on a still day with the wind in the right direction, could be heard a mile or two away. In dry summer weather its progress was marked by a rolling 'smoke-screen' of dust that trailed through the countryside in its wake, far longer and denser than was raised by ordinary forms of horse-drawn transport, short of a battery of the Royal Horse Artillery at full gallop.

At last the motorcar comes into view round a bend, with frantic tooting of its squeeze-bulb horn, juddering visibly, and with its enormous brass, carbide head-lamps and scarcely smaller oil side-lamps glistening in the sunlight. Since this form of transport was still thought of as a horseless carriage, it was of elevated construction, with the back seat usually a little higher than the front one, and signposts were correspondingly high. Passengers enjoyed not only unobstructed vision ahead, but a view of the countryside over all but the highest hedges, which is denied to the *ventre-a-terre* motorist of today. A woman motorist was usually enveloped in a long dust-cloak, or its winter equivalent. A hat was *de rigeur* and most likely of a sort which I can only describe as a large double-crumpet with a big button on top, providing an anchorage for the two constituent parts of a motoring veil, tied in a big, floppy bow under the chin. It served both to protect the wearer's complexion and to keep the hat on in the open car. It was not necessary to own, or even to ride in, a motorcar to wear this status-symbol headgear. The driver, usually a dashing young fellow or a more elderly Romeo, wore a peaked cloth cap (not the 'duncher', but the more closely fitting kind with a little button on top) back to front, with heavy goggles. This gave both passengers and apprehensive pedestrians a striking impression of daring driving at speed, perhaps all of thirty miles an hour. Rapid development was taking place in the motor industry, and the changes between 1910 and 1914 were dramatic, at least as noted by a small boy.

Motor-cycles were seen more frequently than motorcars on country roads, and quite often they were used by enterprising newspaper reporters – unless I gained that impression from Lynn Doyle's *Ballygullion* rather than from my own unaided memory. They were primitive machines, with the old fashioned cycle frame and pedals still prominent features. They had a belt drive which was liable to slip, so that from the very beginning the tendency was for motorcyclists to ride in anxious contemplation of the back wheel. There was also a tendency to carry 'dog-bombs', small, fairly harmless stun-bombs, to scare off the dogs that in those days invariably attacked a motorcycle on sight. The motorcyclist's garb in all seasons comprised a heavy, knee-length, macintosh coat with a formidable belt of rubber or leather links, macintosh trousers-cum-gaiters, back to front 'duncher' with goggles, and huge leather gauntlets. The young men led an excessively strenuous life, spending a considerable part of their time in pushing their machines at an indignant lop-sided jog-trot, punctuated by violent back-firing, in an effort to start them, the kick-starter not yet having come into use. When the rider accomplished this he had, hampered by clumsy protective clothing, to vault lightly into the saddle before the stuttering engine stalled. It was then essential to pedal frantically until it began to run freely and, just as his strength seemed bound to fail, he was triumphantly under power in a fog of exhaust smoke.

Here let me add a footnote on the earliest motor horn. When I first rode in a motorcar, about 1908, the thing that most excited my envious admiration, apart of course from the fabulous vehicle itself, was the instrument, now long forgotten, which the chauffeur blew at every bend, as though rounding the walls of Jericho. I do not know whether this was a primitive, pre-squeeze-bulb horn, or some kind of French variant or American aberration. By dint of much hopeful wishing, in which I had become fairly expert, having developed a sound, though not infallible instinct about the limits of practicability, I was given a small model of this remarkable instrument for myself. It consisted of a vulcanite mouthpiece, as for holding gigantic cigars or for some large musical instrument, broadening down to something about the diameter of a table-napkin-ring. To the lower rim was fastened a length of some two or three inches of thin rubber tubing of the same diameter. From a similar but considerably larger instrument of joy the chauffeur had produced a note like that of a bull in pain or a liner in a fog. From my model there emerged a raspberry, but how splendid a raspberry! Have our avant garde composers and orchestrators perhaps missed something? Surely there is room for a *cor framboise*.

It must have been about 1909 or 1910 that I suffered the bitterest disappointment of my life. There was a young man, about whom I had heard a great deal, and because of his adventurous deeds had installed in my personal pantheon as 'Ferguson the Fearless'. This was Mr Harry Ferguson, well known many years later as a designer and manufacturer of advanced types of engines, racing cars and, in a more utilitarian way, tractors. He had announced his intention of making an ascent in his flying machine – one did not, as yet, just take off in a plane – from the sands of Newcastle, Co. Down, on an advertised date.

It seemed, when the great day arrived, that the entire population of every barony in the County and from every art, had taken the day off to witness this epoch-making event. If the beautiful Miss Bradys went in their private ass and cart as they did to Phil the Fluter's Ball, I can only say that they were very lucky. I was taken by my parents, along with the inevitable relatives and friends, in a special excursion train. I think my elders were congratulating themselves on the fact that our party more than filled a carriage, but 'sitting familiar', we settled down without much discomfort. Then, suddenly, the door burst open and the public surged in like the sea. They stood on our toes, they sat on our knees, they climbed into the luggage racks and crawled under the seats, or at least that was what it seemed like. Groucho, Chico and Harpo Marx and their hilarious gag-man, S J Perelman, were not, thank goodness, present in the flesh, especially the first mentioned, but they were surely there in spirit. We were participating in what might have been a full dress rehearsal for a characteristic situation in all Marx Brothers films a quarter of a century in the future. At last the door was shut by the exertions of a burly porter and we were off.

We arrived at our destination relatively undamaged, but the more elderly members of our party with (might one say?) their 'horse feathers' decidedly ruffled. We were borne on the human tide from the station to the sands, where mounted constabulary were already riding range like cowboys with a herd of Texas Longhorns. The happy licensee of a refreshment tent in the dunes was assured of a golden harvest (and it would have been gold then) if only the poles and guy-ropes could take the strain of sea winds and thirsty customers, determined to miss neither refreshments not the ascent of Mr Ferguson. There, sure enough, was the fabulous plane on the strand. It was a delicate construction of slender struts and stays, only the wings covered with fragile fabric and all else wide open, including the pilot's seat, which I think was in front of the engine, and the whole contraption was mounted on bicycle wheels.

The site for the ascent was probably chosen because of its natural, sandy runway. At that precise point 'The Mountains of Mourne sweep down to the sea', accompanied, I am sure, on a windy day by treacherous, gusty down-draughts, which would probably have been dangerous for such a flimsy, feebly powered aircraft. High in the air a box kite, very similar in construction to the flying-machine itself, was soaring and swooping madly in the stiff breeze. After watching its antics for an unconscionable time and testing the pull on the string as anxiously as ever did Benjamin Franklin, Mr Ferguson decisively hauled the kite down and announced that there would be no flight that day after all. An old silent film caption would certainly have stated: 'It's murder, Colonel, I tell you, to send the kid up in that crate.'

There came from the crowd such a sound, as when the visiting team puts a fast one into the net. The family tactician moved us to the right, or landward, flank for fear of being crowded into the sea. The Royal Irish Constabulary, horse and foot, tightened their chinstraps and prepared to sell their lives dearly. There was no need . If there was anything revolutionary in that situation, apart from the incipient conquest of the air, it was *Marxiste tendence Groucho*.

VI

ORDER

$\mathcal{T}$he Police Barracks – despite the name, an ordinary enough looking dwelling-house – was less than a hundred yards from our garden. I was therefore aware of the comings and goings of the policeman, and well aware also that they were of interest to the local girls and *vice-versa*. They were indeed big well-set-up young men, and if not exactly Adonises, they had nicely nurtured moustaches. I think their posting was probably arranged in accordance with a principle which, in the ancient Roman Empire, sent troops raised on one of its provinces to serve in another. It seemed that the Royal Irish Constabulary may have sent big, husky fellows from the Black North to serve in Leinster, Munster and Connacht. While the patrolling of patches in Ulster may have been entrusted to big bosthoons from the deep South and far West.

The men of this force were not ostensibly armed on duty. The heavy service revolver on a lanyard, buttoned into its holster and obviously unsuited to a fast Wild-West draw, came in with 'The Troubles' and the Royal *Ulster* Constabulary. It is true that the R I C constable's truncheon was not carried in a special trousers pocket, like that of an English bobby, but in a cylindrical scabbard attached to the black leather belt, which also bore a pouch, rather like that which used to be strapped to the back of a bicycle saddle, and which I suppose carried handcuffs. I have always assumed that the tubular scabbards held truncheons but, for all I know, individual examples may have held telescopes, or jumbo sticks of peppermint rock, or certificates of the freedom of Derry, or even two or three small Guinnesses. On ordinary duty the constables wore flat, peaked caps, but on special occasions they assumed an impressive grandeur. Then they wore spiked helmets, more like those of the old British Infantry of the Line than the helmets of English police. These made them look at least seven-and-a-half feet tall, and their neatly rolled capes, slung over a shoulder in the old infantry fashion, added to their military appearance. Officers were trim in rifle green, with immaculately boned and polished brown boots and leggings.

Occasionally Brass of a much higher rank than that of District Inspector made his appearance, the sword of ceremony by his side. In my mind I identified this officer with Bobs, Field Marshal Lord Roberts of Kandahar, the military hero of the days of my childhood before the Great War. I had seen in a history of the Boer War, by Sir Arthur Conan Doyle, a picture of the pocket paladin at Paardeberg receiving the surrender of a shambling General Cronje. The visiting police officer's cocky stance and bearing strongly resembled that of the Field Marshal. Could there, I wondered a little uneasily, be a Cronje in the neighbourhood, or could our name be mistaken for it? There was indeed a military air about those little local inspections. Perhaps my memory deceives me in depicting a scene in which a prisoner was being taken away on an outside, or 'jaunting,' car, escorted by two burly constables, or perhaps warders, with carbines.

Recalling the old-time constabulary reminds me sharply of the shock evinced by my parents, one morning at breakfast, on learning that on the previous evening 'some of the boys' had lain in wait for someone well known locally. It seemed that only the intervention of the parish priest prevented a murderous attack. This may seem commonplace nowadays. It was not yet the case in about 1910, despite the old sporting gun in Carrickfergus Castle, with one barrel inscribed 'Snipe' and the other 'Landlords'. I am not sure whether or not the inscriptions are of the same date as the gun. They might have been engraved at the behest of a later sportsman.

I suppose it was the exuberance of the Saturday night drunks, more than anything else, which ensured that the police earned their pay. The inebriate, about to run amok, usually gave a great 'ghuldher', or gorilla-like yell, and more often than not, the challenge was taken up by at least one fellow reveller. Fights were commonplace, for drink was astonishingly cheap by present day standards, and the police had their work cut out for them. There have been many descriptions of Saturday-night drinking; here is another, quoted because it fits in so exactly with strangers' ideas of Ulster. It should be explained the Mr

MacNeill, called 'Knock 'em Down' was a well-known hotelier and publican in Larne:

> *'Knockem had a good idea for clearin' the house when it was gettin' late on a Sathurday night, an' they wus jist bletherin' an' talkin'. He w'uld eye the crowd over an' see what soart o' crowd it wus. When he thought he hed it sized up, he w'uld call a fella over an' ask him til go outside an' curse the Pope or King William as the case might be. Then, when the rush started, he w'uld say 'g' night bhoys, Ah'll be seein' ye Monda', and shlap the dhoor on them'.*

Here, from the same racy, nautical source, Bob Nelson of happy memory, Harbourmaster of Portaferry, an old shellback and Royal Naval Reservist, is a splendid description of a fight, at once graphic, comprehensive and succinct, It must have occurred in the mid nineteenth century, when Bob's father's little coasting vessel was lying at Quoile Quay, near Downpatrick. This is no Saturday night free-for-all, but an affair of honour. The sailor, Sleith, is a peaceable fellow and a reluctant combatant; Madeen, the landsman, is a professional pugilist:

> *'. . . . . So Sleith sayed, if it must be, they'd bether git at it an' git it over, an' so they went ashore. Now Sleith wus a fella that wus all bones an' as hard as nails, an' he hadn't as much flesh on him as w'uld bait a mousethrap. So they started in an' fell to, an' after the first roun' they stud the boxer Madeen agin a bollard an' give him a dhrink av' watther, an' afther the secon' roun' they tuk him home in a kert, an' that finished that'.*

In Katesbridge there was an Orange Hall, but I cannot remember what it looked like. Such buildings were seldom notable for the elegance of their architecture. There was also of course, an Orange band, of which it would have been impossible to be unaware, loud as it was with drumfire 'and the vile squealing of the wryneck'd fife'. Was it the instrument or the player that was wryneck'd in Shakespeare's time? The fife, as an instrument, seem to me a little inflexible. The repertoire of that band of music, as of others like it, was limited not only by instrumental and personal factors and the time available for practice, but also by religious and political exigencies as well. What was required of it was music redolent of Protestant orthodoxy and political steadfastness, reminiscent of Derry, Aughrim and the Boyne. In addition, full allowance had to be made for the limitations of fingering by toil-stiffened hands and the vagaries of breath-control, especially under the influence of malt liquor. 'Ye'r merry the day Sammy.' 'Aye, but man, ye sh'uld see me when Ah hev nine inches av porther in me!' Full as a fifer was a proverbial saying. Few, if any, of the great composers seem to have worked with precisely this concatenation of requirements in mind. The usual result, apart from offensive partizan songs like 'Croppies Lie Down', was apt to be something like 'Hold the Fort for I am Coming', suggestive of King William marching to the relief of some stronghold hard pressed by the Redskins. Oh well, it was much the same kind of idea! Two boys, Jack and Bobby, with whom I occasionally chatted through the bars, were entrusted with the solemn responsibility for, respectively, the cymbals and the triangle, contributing a touch of eastern militarism to the march, heightened by the Drum Major's masterful and athletic handling of his ornamental knobkerry. They were just as happy playing the children to their Sunday school 'feet' as the Lodge to the solemnities of 'The Twalfth'.

The other side naturally had a band too and, more gifted musically it may be, theirs was a brass affair, I think. The celebrations it accompanied, as observed from a discreet distance on top of the Mound, seem in long retrospect to have been peaceful enough, combining the characteristics of a liturgical procession and a reunion of old comrades of Brian Boru. The whole affair seems to me, in retrospect, to have had the identical air of conscientious, if misconceived, political antiquarianism and religious fervour as did the processions of those who 'dug with the other foot'. In this case the march was accompanied by the melancholy romanticism of 'The Wearing of the Green', and by the heart-searing rending by 'The Minstrel Boy' of harp-strings so tense that they were liable to go pop at any moment. The participants appeared to be a pretty innocuous lot of country folk, rather than a sinister organization preparing for bloodthirsty rebellion and massacre. The Irish Nationalists were still striving for Home Rule by peaceful, constitutional methods, and it was a time of high hopes for them. The procession I have in mind must have been in 1910; that was the year when an atmosphere of political ferment was created by two general elections within a twelvemonth, Lloyd George's contentious budget and the prospect of a spectacular constitutional crisis at Westminster over the vetoing power of the House of Lords, and was intensified by the death of King Edward VII, the succession of the inexperienced George V, and the expectation of a new Home Rule Bill. I still remember the buzz of excitement in and around a lighted polling station, as I passed it with my father in the dusk of a winter evening.

Perhaps it was not surprising that the peaceful, Nationalist demonstrators, of that time, burned my father in effigy, along with such other notorious characters as King William and the opponent (unsuccessful, if my memory is not at fault) of Mr Jerry McVeigh, the Nationalist candidate in South Down. That my father should be thus ritually combusted, and in such company, seemed to amuse rather than disturb him. It struck me, a six-year-old, as a very disconcerting impertinence, and I am sure my mother saw it in the same light. All this must have given me furiously to think, for it was my first intimation, dimly understood, that things were happening which threatened the security of my smug little world.

VII

METROPOLIS

A visit to Belfast often meant a stay with my widowed paternal grandmother. At the Great Northern terminus, a typical piece of railway classicism with a dumpily Doric-pillared portico, then in Great Victoria Street, we piled into a frowsty four-wheeler smelling of musty hay, old leather, oats and porter. I would have preferred a smartly trotting hansom, such as the youngest and most dashing of my uncles used, but that was not at all the conveyance for even a small family with all the luggage then considered necessary for a short stay. I think my mother's dresses travelled in a large basketwork trunk covered with some kind of shiny fabric, such as 'American cloth', her hats in a large, round hatbox, and my father's silk hat in a leather container specially designed for this still indispensable article.

We rumbled along sedately over the stone squaresetts, in which were laid the rails for the grinding, clanging, swaying, open-topped electric tramcars. Motorcars and taxis were still very few, even three or four years before the Great War. The pervading sounds were those of rumbling and rattling wheels, jangling trams, hoofbeats – some slow and ponderous, some light and swift – and the jingling and creaking of harness. Rising piercingly above this groundswell of noise, the melancholy yells of newsboys proclaimed the national dailies – 'Skeätchameälamirror' – and the Belfast evening paper – 'Tellyellyseaxth'[4]. The air was polluted, not by the fumes of the internal combustion engine, but by gritty coal smoke from domestic hearths and tall factory chimneys, blighting the sunshine, begriming the rain and sulphurating the fog.

Respectively, 'Daily Sketch' and Daily Mirror' and (Belfast) Telegraph, Early Sixth (edition)'.

51

A characteristically pungent-smell from a distillery, the Old Cromac, I suppose, was offensive to me as a child. The distillery itself disappeared before I had any interest in its products. The smell was quite unlike the coffee aroma from Guinnesses on a sunny morning in Dublin, which was still the capital city and visited accordingly, but occasionally just in passing through from the Holyhead boat when the Irish port was still Kingstown. One of the most impressive sights amid the Belfast traffic, in that penultimate phase of horse-drawn vehicles, was a brewers' dray with its superb greys or chestnuts glossily groomed, the burly driver and his brawny mate with rich complexions aglow, bowler-hatted and enthroned in lordly dignity, the whole equipage an embodiment of goodness and strength, as advertised.

The City of Belfast had changed its Georgian look not so very long before this time. My father remembered a mainly Georgian town in his schooldays, about 1875-85. A good deal of regrettable destruction must have taken place in the name of progress, as it still does everywhere, but progress to what? The fine old Linen Hall was ruthlessly eradicated, leaving only the name of a dreary, depressing, little-used street (that is as I last saw it in the 1930s) to commemorate dignity departed. The City Fathers, in the early years of the twentieth century, already installed in the present Mughal palace, from which the gorgeous East might have been held in fee, were presiding over a booming metropolis of linen, engineering and shipbuilding, The owners of some of the larger department stores (for the supermarket was not yet) had a similar rush of imperial grandeur to the head. The city had consequently seen a certain limited efflorescence of what Sir Osbert Lancaster classified as 'Edwardian Baroque' architecture, with its whopping proportions and hypertrophied decoration. A few dignified buildings escaped a face-lift and some old street names survived, like the sweet old Sugarhouse Entry, where I always wanted to go as a child, but never did. The authorities in the world of education, less Philistine, or at least much less wealthy, than city magnates, did not display architectural megalomania. The Royal Belfast Academical Institution, that is dear, familiar 'Inst.', had half its honest, grimy Georgian façade concealed behind a cupola-enriched and, I suppose, civically-endowed Technical College neighbour. Perhaps 'The Black Man', statue of the formidable Dr Henry Cooke in the street fronting the pair is denouncing the outrage. Farther out from the City Centre, the old Queen's College (still so called for many years, although it achieved independent university status in 1908) had a quasi-Tudor or Jacobean façade with a Magdalen tower. This pile, which might so easily have been a painful monstrosity, had happily become a mellow example of early Victorian Redbrick, a distinguished seat of learning, as also of endearing academic eccentricity.

I may have conveyed the impression that, in the first decade of the twentieth century, Belfast was a city of brash Department stores. This was far from the case, for in fact they were relatively few. There were numerous more modest establishments where customers were waited upon, as in the big stores, individually, with courtesy, good manners and quite superhuman patience. The word 'ducks' was not a form of address in public, but confined to poulterers' shops, and 'luv' was not commonly bandied about. The fussy customer at, let us say, a haberdashery counter, who had come to buy half a yard of ribbon, seated herself firmly in a high chair by the counter, just as people nowadays sit on bar stools, but less casually, in an upright, no-nonsense posture. She would expect to monopolise, until her requirements had been met exactly, the services of an assistant, summoned by a frock-coated shopwalker with a 'Forward, Miss Smith', like Napoleon launching a charge of cuirassiers. I do not suggest that this was a socially desirable situation, pleasant though it was to be so served, but simply record that it is how shopping was done in the old days before the two World Wars.

With my father I often visited a shrine, for one felt that it was no less, where a hierophant of Nicotine made up Jimmy's own smoking mixture with nice attention to the exact proportions of Virginia, Latikaea and Perique, weighted to a scruple in just the kind of scales that Justice herself holds. I think that tobacco cost eightpence an ounce, perhaps a shade expensive by the standards of that time but, in present-day terms, an incredible 51p a pound. The transaction took only a few minutes, and the contrast of this with the hypothetical haberdashery counter makes it clear why I so much preferred accompanying my father rather than my mother. There was a good deal of boredom for a small boy in either case, but with Father there were interesting interludes. Too much time, I considered, was taken up in new and second-hand bookshops and in looking at pictures. I liked a group of seedy little shops in Castle Lane long before it was first redeveloped. Cheek by jowl with a second-hand bookshop were a pet shop, with many kinds of cage-birds and small animals, and a fascinating little junk shop. While the books engaged Father, I could while away a little of the time by inspecting the other emporia.

I do not know what my first cinema programme comprised (not at all Father's kind of pictures) but I remember seeing the film of King George V's Coronation. In this all the wheels seemed to revolve backwards, while the Yeomen of the Guard accompanying the State Coach marched at an excessively fast Rifleman's pace. I saw this film again many years later, whether at the time of George VI's Coronation or that of our present Sovereign Lady I do not remember. The wheels still revolved backwards.

I best remember a day when we went to the docks and began by admiring a big windjammer that was unloading maize. A very few years later I would have identified her as a four masted barque and have known better how to admire her. These lovely things had not much longer to ply the oceans under the red ensign. Having paid our respects to the old charmer, we crossed the Harbour in the Ha'penny Ferry to admire a new one. Our ears assaulted by the deafening, heavy machine-gun clatter of the rivetters' hammers in the shipyards of Workman – Clarke and Harland and Wolff, we made our way to the fitting-out berth of the latter yard. There, almost ready for her sea trials, lay the pride of the White Star Line, RMS *Olympic*. A year or so later I was taken to view her new sister ship, RMS *Titanic* before she set out for her maiden Atlantic voyage from Southampton to Davy Jones. It was a great disappointment, after all the publicity, for her additional thousand gross tons were not visible to my naked eye, nor were the elegant appointments that made her the most sumptuous as well as the largest and latest work in naval architecture.

Economic considerations of cargo space and passenger accommodation were, by that time, resulting in rather slab-sided hulls both for sail and for steam. When the keels of these great White Star liners and those of their Cunard and German competitors were laid, the ideal passenger ship was a seagoing Versailles or Schönbrunn, powered by prepotent turbines and propelled by triple screws. Their sole function was to provide the fastest possible passages, in the most sybaritic surroundings, for international financiers and arms dealers, diamond magnates and dollar millionaires, titled passengers in search of marriageable American heiresses and *vice-versa*. The famous naval architect and engineer of the previous century, Isambard Kingdom Brunel, must have worn a belt as well as braces – just in case; certainly in his nautical monster, the *Great Eastern*, he provided paddle wheels as well as a screw and half a dozen masts for the same reason. His early twentieth-century successors went in for funnels in a big way. Publicity usually involved a picture of one such funnel lying on its side in some well-known site, such as Whitehall, Donegall Place or Unter den Linden, with a couple of tramcars or buses passing each other inside. Three such funnels seemed to form a quorum, four were pretentious, but five were positively vulgar, even by Edwardian standards, and liable to de derided as 'The Packet O'Woodbines'. These 'Ocean Greyhounds', as some imaginatively stimulated pressman described them, combining spectacularly the qualities of the Whippet and the St Bernard, competed for 'The Blue Riband of the Atlantic'. Their boiler-room crews of hard-case stokers must have sweated their souls out to fire the monsters across the ocean. Yet it is the song *'My Old Man's a Fireman on an Elder-Dempster Boat'* that commemorates the sea-going stoker.'

The leisurely procedure of shopping with my Mother, when I was very small, made me dance, in the literal sense of the word, with frustration. There was one shop, a much too frequent port of call, that I dreaded above all, although I was shown the greatest possible kindness there. This was a fashionable little hat shop belonging to my charming, but very formidable, aunt, Dolly Cronne. Why she chose to be called Dolly, I really do not know, for her name was Sarah or Sally, and it would have been difficult to imagine anyone less dolly-like. She could never have been a stay-at-home Miss. She was a generously built, handsome woman in rather a masculine way, with red-gold hair. This was emphasised by her choice, among the female fashions of the early twentieth century, of those that copied men's styles, which I suppose were symbols of coveted emancipation. Dolly needed no emancipating; she had an air of command combined with the gift of blarney. Ordinarily she was kindness itself and extravagantly generous, but if provoked, she had a fiery temper and a flow of furious eloquence which, with no holds barred, made her utterly

---

' *An approximation to its opening lines goes like this:– My old man's a Fireman on an Elder-Dempster boat. He wears gorblimey trousers and a gorblimey hat, And he wears a something muffler around his something throat – Oh, my old man's a Fireman on an Elder-Dempster boat!*

devastating. The eruption was over as quickly as had arisen. She never apologised, but well knew how to soothe her victims' ruffled feelings. Unsurprisingly, she never married and her deepest devotion was to her young brother, Fred.

Dolly's shop was in the Queen's Arcade and this, in spite of unending pedestrian traffic, had the effect, at once echoing and muted, of a cathedral nave. It created for me an atmosphere of melancholy resignation. There were two saleswomen, or ought I to say, more grandly *vendeuses?* (Not, I think in Ulster!) These Dolly addressed by surnames only, as she did all her employees. Up a wrought-iron spiral stair was a large room with a huge half-moon window, which diffused such light as filtered through the glass roof of the Arcade. This was supplemented by electric bulbs of the primitive pattern with shark's-teeth filaments. There was a gas fire, no less primitive, distributing impartially warmth and effluvium, and a gas ring with a perpetually simmering kettle. I do not know whether this was used only for the brewing of tea, or whether the steam was needed in the process of shaping hats. Grouped in a wide, sociable semi-circle round the window on hard, round-bottomed chairs of the kind with perforated seats for the aeration of the sedentarily employed, were some six sewing women and girl apprentices, chattering sixteen to the dozen. They were surrounded by skeleton hats, and hatboxes. A big table was deeply littered with what Eliza Dolittle called 'the whole of Kew Gardens', not to mention Covent Garden Market and the Zoological Society's aviaries. I think only fish were excluded from the decorative materials, though an embroidered gudgeon, such as Isaac Walton described, might have lent a quiet air of distinction to a hat.

The choosing of a hat by a customer, back in 1909 or thereabouts, seemed to me an excessively elaborate and lengthy ritual. Madame's dress or tailor-made costume (ie suit) or coat had first to be examined with care, so as to establish the correct texture and colour for the hat, at least provisionally. Then the lengthy process began with the very careful choice of a basic framework of straw or felt or velvet or buckram, or whatever it might be, both fashionable and becoming the customer in shape. This was of fundamental importance and it involved a good deal of manipulation. After this a brief break was indicated, with perhaps a cup of tea. Then began the real fun, the decoration of the hat which, as in the game of snakes and ladders, often resulted in a return to square one. Combinations of ribbon, flowers, foliage, feathers and fruits of the earth, as well as of the giddy imagination of the manufacturers of these trimmings, followed each other until the customer's ideal was achieved, or an impasse had been reached. At that psychological moment Miss Cronne herself might intervene, sweeping everything aside and producing the individual confection of moonshine that she had already, in all probability, decided upon for the customer. The latter, having effected some running repairs with what was called *papier poudré*, for the powder compact did not yet seem to be much in evidence, departed. The new creation, pinned together as it was, passed upstairs to be stitched and finished in the form of no mere florist's, but a combined seedsman's and taxidermist's bouquet, in which some lyre-bird, quetzalcoatl or phoenix had nested. I should think the fire risk, both for

'*The Hat*'

premises and hats, was considerable.

The girl who stayed at home with Grandmama was Katie. She was plainer and built on even more generous lines than her younger sister. Unlike her, she had raven hair, as I first remember her. Lacking Dolly's fire, her eloquence was employed more gently. Good manners and correct behaviour were important in her view and she insisted upon them in a quiet, kindly way. This she combined, incongruously it might seem, with a rumbustious sense of humour,

Authentication of the Hat

57

which could reduce the family when they were alone, for she was shy in company, to tears of helpless laughter. Like the rest of them, she doted on her youngest, yet unmarried, brother Fred and spoilt him outrageously.

My grandmother seemed to me a dignified, composed and immensely old lady, although she did not wear on top of her head the little round lace or crocheted mat (for I can think of no more appropriate term) that many old ladies affected in those days. Their present day successors of similar age would probably be driving their cars, instead of sitting by the fire, and fit to pass as the elder sisters of their grand-daughters. My grandmother had once been a lively, merry person, but as I remember her in her sombre widow's weeds, suffering seemed to have engraved its marks on her face. I think she considered that the régime imposed by my parents was a trifle severe, for 'let the wee fellow enjoy himself' was her motto where I was concerned. She did her best to ensure it by arranging various treats when we stayed with her. She was a confirmed tipper of grandchildren with golden sovereigns and half sovereigns and big silver crowns. Tips of such magnitude were really of little use to me, for my mother was sure to put them away for me, a proceeding which I deeply resented, having inherited a very different tradition. I greatly preferred a sixpenny or shilling tip, which I was allowed to keep, and what a lordly spending spree one could have then with a 'tanner' or a 'bob' in a confectioner's shop!

Fred was a big, handsome buck, but unlike James Joyce's Buck Mulligan (alias Oliver St John Gogarty) he could not recite Greek verse, for his heart was more in the rugger field than in the sports of the Odyssey. He was unmistakably a buck in the old Irish tradition, a man of fastidiousness and splendid courage. He was the most genial of men and had a way with him, especially with the girls, even in old age when crippled by a stroke. Fred had an inestimable gift of commanding instant attention and eager service wherever he went. No foreign language was ever an impediment to him, although he spoke none correctly. A comrade-in-arms early in the Great War described a scene when a lot of Jocks were crowding round a farmhouse door trying to persuade the farmer's wife to let them have some eggs. Up came Fred, pushing them all aside with a sweep of his arms and stepped into the kitchen, saying 'regardez-moi, madame. Je suis l'homme!' He clearly was and the eggs were forthcoming.

Fred was known as 'Casey' in his beloved Black Watch, 'more a religion

Paddy Newel and Fred. Cronne,
6th Black Watch (T), 1914.

than a regiment'. He and a group of his friends had joined as Territorials, when such battalions were raised in, I think, 1909, after the Army reforms of 1907. It was fashionable and a splendid lark then, and I daresay the old full-dress scarlet and the waggle o' the kilt were believed to give the girls a thrill in those simple old times. The year 1915 brought tragedy to that little group. Paddy Newell, Fred's closest friend, was mortally wounded, at Levantie. Fred brought him in under fire and was commissioned on the field. His friend Billy Fraser and others were killed in the Battle of Loos later in the same year. Fred survived the war. He claimed to have been the first British officer on the Somme. Wounded, he was attached to Scottish Command for a time. He ended the war in Macedonia where, at one end of the scale, he mounted a guard of honour for the King of Serbia, at the other was invited to a wild-boar hunt by an Albanian bandit with whom, characteristically, he had made friends. Fred's stories were all basically true, but elaborated with such rococo abandon that one took them with a large grain of salt. In his last years, he claimed that he could become a Freeman of the City of London any day. That for a yarn, we all thought, but after his death the certificate was found, ready to be presented to the City Chamberlain.

In 1939, at the age of 53 and no longer on the Reserve of Officers, he contrived to get himself commissioned in the RAFVR, probably through the influence of his old comrade Air Vice-Marshal Tyrell. To his great disappointment he was used merely as DAPM, but he did get himself air-borne and involved in a crash, which did him no good. Too kind-hearted and a poor judge of his fellow men, he inevitably died badly off. Fred did much for me, introducing me to a good tailor, shoemaker and many of the good things of life, and also to a number of expensive tastes. The best would do! I am proud to have been regarded more as a friend than a nephew.

VIII

PISGAH

The early summer of the vintage year 1911 – also note-worthy for the Agadir Incident and the Parliament Act – saw us in a new home in Portaferry, on the Ards Peninsula, near the mouth of Strangford Lough. It was a Georgian sea-front house, the outward aspect of which, like that of its neighbour on the north side, was marred, at least for purists, by the addition of Victorian bay windows. Its Regency neighbour on the south side was not destined to be similarly defaced, for its windows were original, for many years to come, but then with the added horror of roughcast. It still preserved, in 1911 and for many years, an elegant, if somewhat over-sanguine, façade. Viewed Baconially ('houses are built to live in, not to look at') or Corbusierwise, the effect of our bay windows was breathtaking. They framed three Tennysonially romantic views: a bar for crossing, marked by a lighthouse, long disused; a rushing tidal version of the wild cataract with wooded shores; castles in quadruplicate, with walls admirably situated for the splendour to fall on them. They are very lovely views and Yeats's Aedh, who wished for the cloths of Heaven, could have found no better place from which to view their sunset hues.

I best like the approach to Portaferry from the sea, as St Patrick found it on his return to Ireland to begin his missionary enterprise, miraculously cleaving the rock that bears his name, when it threatened him with shipwreck. Perhaps the saint had a lubberly crew to try his patience, when he was in no mood to brook obstacles. The Vikings came that way too in their longships, either exulting in the speed with which the flood tide bore them in, or sweating at their oars with a 'yuch-hey-saa-saa' if they had arrived at the bar on an ebb tide.

They, however, were fine seamen, who could cope with the situation without having to resort to cleaving rocks. They could easily have run their longships ashore on Ballyhornan Strand outside the Lough to wait for the flood to make. This would have afforded them an agreeable, and perhaps marginally profitable, opportunity to attack the little settlement of Kilclief from the rear. They are recorded as having sacked it at least once.

One can see quite clearly why the Vikings gave the great sea lough with its long, narrow entrance, the fittingly descriptive name of *Strang Fjord* instead of the Gaelic *Cuan*, meaning a harbour or haven and implying something very much more placid than it is. They also named the so-called whirlpool (although it is not precisely that) off Bankmore 'The Routen (snoring) Wheels'. The entrance of the Lough is some five miles long and, in some parts, not much over half a mile wide. Relative to the size of the Lough, it resembles the neck of a Burgundy bottle, and the tides rush through it in furious spate, hazardous in the extreme to ignorant, inexperienced or foolhardy navigators.

The rock inside the bar, with its disused lighthouse, was named Rock Anguish on some early maps. Later it appears as Rock Angus, and local fishermen referred to it, with a Gaelic-sounding inflexion, as Rock 'n Gus or more familiarly The Goose. It is not at all a place where, in ordinary circumstances, a wildfowler would seek his quarry; and this all goes to show how very misleading place-names can be. The original name was probably Irish for the rock has a tiny inlet, which may have given it the name *angCuas* (Goose) Rock of the cove. When a gale opposes the powerful tides and great waves leap up the lighthouse, as in some contemporary illustration of Grace Darling's exploit, the bar becomes a surging fury and the narrows a frothing maelstrom, into which, one would think, no mariner in his senses would enter, especially under sail. Yet, as a small boy, I saw on the beach where it had been towed in, the battered and waterlogged afterdeck, still in one piece, of the little schooner *Loughlong* whose master was foolhardy enough to try to bring her into port in such conditions. That was all, save a few broken spars, that was ever seen again of the trim little ship and her crew.

When you come in on the flood on a fine morning, with an eight or ten knot tide under you, the dominant feature, five miles to the north, is a shoulder of hill heaving itself above the hanging woods of Portaferry House. It is over three-hundred feet high, a giant among the little, rolling porpoise hills that give the district its partly Anglicised name of the Ards, heights by the Eastern Sea in early Irish chronicles. This hill was therefore called 'The Mountain'. On the summit of this Pisgah, long ago, an old fellow called Moses Warnock caused a stone platform to be built, from which to 'view the landscape o'er'. It is well worth the gentle climb to 'stand where Moses stood', for there are superb views extending round the full three hundred and sixty degrees of the compass. One does not view things from so great a height as to make nearer objects look remote and unreal. From south, through east, to north sweeps a great arc of the Irish Sea, with the mountains of the Isle of Man, high on the eastern horizon, drawing away the rain clouds, as those of Mourne draw them south west, leaving this favoured spot under the clearer skies between. To the north-east the Mull of Galloway lies low on the sea's rim.

In 1911, when I first saw the view, that stretch of sea was full of shipping, great and small, and much of it still under sail. Numbers of little coastal schooners and ketches and fishing luggers were to be seen every day, and quite often at least one full-rigged ship, or more likely four-masted barque, as well as coastal and ocean-going steam-ships, was in sight. I remember, a good many years later and not on that spot, the roughest, toughest old salt of my acquaintance gazing with brimming eyes at the lovely *Herzogin Cecilie,* beating up the Irish Sea, and saying in hushed tones 'Och, yer lovely! Ah wisht Ah wus in ye.' It was, in its way, an even more heartfelt, certainly more knowledgeable, and as true an appreciation of a ship's beauty

> *As thou, aslant with trim tackle and shrouding,*
> *From the proud nostril curve of a prow's line,*
> *In the offing scattering foam, thy white sails crowding*

Yet Hughie must have suffered much hardship and privation in his seagoing days in sail. He claimed to have rounded the Horn in a pair of beaded slippers, the gift of Dr MacDonald ('A dacent man; Divil recaive the betther!') which he had been wearing when he was 'crimped' on the Chile coast, at Callao, or it may have been Iquique. The point of his story was that, thus handicapped, he won fulsome praise from the cracking-on Master, who 'dam' near had the sticks out av her', and the bully, bucko Mate for his prime seamanship. The tales of this Aedh (which is Hugh) and the sailcloths he handed on his voyages were as colourful as the improbable slippers.

Looking north-west, the distant view is blocked by the Castlereagh and Holywood Hills. Farther west and south-west are all the drumlins, the little hills of Down, with our old home in Katesbridge and the Bann hidden in their midst. The blue cone of Slieve Crop, mother of the Lagan, indicates the site where the United Irishman, Henry Munro of Lisburn and his force came to grief in '98 in the battle of Ballynahinch. Downpatrick itself is out of sight and so is Drumderg where, in Maytime 1260, the insensate pride and high romantic heroism of Brian O Neill, fighting the wrong battle in the wrong place, led the flower of Gaelic Ulster and that of Connacht under Aedh O Connor, unarmoured, to rout and disaster against the apprehensive, but better equipped English colonists. Brian perished but Aedh survived. Then in the south-west, the Mountains of Mourne sweep down to the sea, looking more impressively beautiful than from almost any other viewpoint that I know. That is the wide panorama: now the nearer one.

To the south lie Killard Point, the 'Goose' with its lighthouse and, a little to the east of it, Ballyquinton Point, the uttermost, desolate end of the Ards Peninsular, the whole of which lies at one's feet. Eastwards is Knockanelder, where the City liner, *City of Lahore*, ran aground hard and fast on the beach, presumably in thick fog. That was in, I think, 1912. We were to see more such wrecks in a few years' time, as a result of the German submarine campaign. I was taken to see the *City of Lahore* by neighbours who were salvage operators; that big steamship was salvaged and so did not end, as yet, in the knacker's yard.

The Ards is a country of rolling hills and raths (ancient farmyard enclosures, many of them, in spite of their romantic fairy folklore) and fertile, well-farmed land. To the south-east, just beyond Portaferry a hill, topped by a windmill tower, is named in Gaelic *Cnoc-na-gobha* (Knocknagow, the smith's hillock) and is probably known now, as it was in my time, as the Windmill Hill. The tower is a useful mark for coastwise mariners. In my boyhood the forge of one of the village's three blacksmiths was just at the bottom of the hill. Windmills were once numerous in the Ards, where streams suitable for watermills are few and insignificant. The village of Portaferry, opposite

Strangford, on a shallow bay on the east side of the narrows of the Lough, is screened from view by woods. Overlooking the modern car-ferry terminal, where once was a small quay, a ruined castle keep used to fly the six lions rampant banner of the Nugent, heirs of the Savages of the Ards, said to have been at one time Seneschals (Stewards) of the Earldom of Ulster, but under which line of earls I do not know. The village square was the scene of an action between the local United Irishmen and a detachment of yeomanry in 1798, of which I will write later. Nearby, in its extensive, demesne, is Portaferry House, a pleasant Georgian country mansion, once the home of General Andrew Nugent, heir of all the Nugents and earlier Savages. It was said at the time of the change of name that 'Old Savage is better than New Gent.' They were kindly people and good servants of the state in war and peace. General Andrew, as a young man, rode with the Inniskillings in the charge of the Heavy Brigade at Balaclava, 'like drops of blood in a dark gray sea.' The great Victorian Poet Laureate also dutifully celebrated Cardigan's spectacular disaster with the Light Brigade, so much more congenial to English sentiment than General Scarlett's remarkable professional triumph with the Heavies. Tennyson's not to reason why. It was sad that the two sons of Sir Roland Nugent died in action with the Irish Guards in Hitler's war, bringing that line to an end in Portaferry.

A few miles northwards from the Mountain is Ardkeen, site of the medieval stronghold of the Savages. Scarcely one stone stands upon another there, not as the result of any military debacle, but because of the spoiling of the deserted castle by the local population for their own purposes. Farther north still, on the eastern shore of the Lough, is Greyabbey where it is said that Affreca sleeps, daughter of Godred, King of Man, and wife of John de Courcy, the first great Anglo-Norman invader of Ulster. Many years ago, I read somewhere that, a century or more ago a plait of her golden hair survived in her tomb, burnished as on the day when she was alive and dead. Close to Greyabbey, at Rosemount, there succeeded one another in my day three elderly brothers of the Montgomery fighting stock, all Generals. 'Could I like Montgomery fight' wrote Burns, 'or gab like Boswell' (who married a Montgomery) some disagreeable characters, whom he did not name, would be dealt with!

Farther along towards Newtownards is Mountstewart, famous for its gardens and lovely vistas of Mourne across the Lough. It was, in my time, the seat of that Marquess of Londonderry known as 'the last of the milords', a tall, slim personage who affected prominent shirt-cuffs and a coat buttoned tightly at an elegant waist – was he not 'Charlie the Cheetah' in Lady Londonderry's imaginary menagerie? Prominent in English as well as in Irish affairs, and at one time Minister for Air, a Punch cartoon carried the tag: 'Britannia alanna, you're Queen of the Ocean/I'll make you the Queen of the Air.' It was a very great pity that he was denied the opportunity to succeed in that enterprise. Lord Londonderry remained a very staunch Ulsterman, like his father before him who, come to think of it, did not die until 1915. It was alleged that the latter had not spoken to his wife, except in public, for the previous thirty years.

Overhanging the muddy head of Strangford Lough is the craggy hill of Scrabo which, tradition used to have it, was the seat of Crocatanty, King of the Irish Fairies. I cannot resist straying, in this connection, far beyond my subject and my competence. His Majesty's name seems to be simply a mispronunciation of the Gaelic words *Cnoc a-tSean-Tighe*, meaning the hill of the old house. Scrabo itself, I should guess, may be *Sceir-both*, crag of the bothy, or, as we might say, of the shanty, Perhaps the association of fairies with the hill may arise from confusion of *sean*, old, with *sidhean*, fairy mound. Scrabo might now be named, with some justification, the hill of the folly, for like 'the castled crag of Drachenfels', it is crowned by a Rhenish tower. This is a monument to Charles Stewart, half-brother of the great Castlereagh, not that at which Byron, who loathed Castlereagh, asked travellers to pause. Charles was the third Marquess of Londonderry, Wellington's dashing Adjutant-General in the Peninsula. The 'horns of Elfland' at Scrabo have long been superseded by those of cars on the Comber road and the neighbouring Bradshaw's Brae, both famous in the TT races of more than half-a-century ago.

In Newtownards, almost within the evening shadow of the craggy old hill, are the miserable ruins of the once famous abbey of *Maghbile* (Movilla) which had associations with St Columba and other great Irish saints and scholars. A few miles to the north of it are such traces as survive of the greatest of all Ireland's distinguished monastic communities, at Bangor. Not very far from Scrabo Hill, on the north-western shore of the Lough, lies Island Mahee, or Nendrum, associated with St Mochai, one of Patrick's earliest disciples. There are to be seen the excavated *cashel* (enclosure) wall, some traces of huts, a very tiny church and the stump of a round tower. It must have been a small community and certainly an early one. Saints and scholars were prominent in the region of Strangford Lough, and so in all ages were the warriors. On Mahee and other islands and also on mainland shores ruins and traces of strongholds of many dates stand, stark and grey, numerous as the priestly herons, whose ubiquitous presence would surely have delighted Dylan Thomas.

There, just below us as we stand on Moses' platform, on the far side of the Lough near the village of Killyleagh, is the motte-like island called Donnan Isle or Dunnyneill, meansing presumably the *dun* or fort of Niall. I do not know which of Ireland's innumerable Nialls he was, but local tradition used firmly to identify him with Niall Noigiallach, (Niall of the Nine Hostages) ancestor of the great kingly dynasty of the Ui Neill. It was even asserted that in this remote spot he confined the nine hostages with whom his name is associated. To me this seems an unlikely story, a piece of fanciful antiquarian romanticising, but ancient tradition is not to be entirely ignored. Be all that as it may, that island earthwork cries out for skilled archaeological investigation before it is further eroded by the tides.

Here, between the Mountain and Dunnyneill, is one of the few areas of relatively open water in this lough of innumerable islands and rocks – 365 they say, inevitably! It is just beyond the full force of the tides that rush through the narrows, a place from which to command movements by ship or boat from every direction. Perhaps it was hereabouts that, in 877, as the Annals of Ulster relate, the fair strangers and the dark, Norwegians and Danes, met in a great sea fight in which the famous Danish Chieftain, Halfdan, was slain. It would not surprise me if a ship burial were found on an island, not necessarily connected with this particular battle, or with another in 926, for there were Norse Settlements and obviously there was much activity in the area of Strangford Lough in the Viking Age.

On the mainland, near Donnyneill, in the village of Killyleagh with its Scottish-baronial castle of the Rowan-Hamiltons, my maternal ancestor, Alexander Sloane, lived. Beyond Killyleagh the broad lands of Clandeboye (the O Neill *Clann na Aedh Buidhe*) stretched deep into north Down and South Antrim. I do not doubt that, in the interests of his Hamilton patron, Alexander exacted payments from the population with scrupulous attention to every 'bawbee', for he was the canny Scottish Receiver of Taxes in Co. Down.

A mile or two south-south-west of Killyleagh is the island-strewn estuary of the Quoile, the wooded river up which St Patrick sailed to Saul, the barn that became the holiest site in Ireland. Farther south a couple of miles begin the beautifully wooded narrows of the Lough, with stately homes. That of Lord Bangor at Castleward, an interesting hermaphrodite construction of Georgian on one side and Strawberry Hill Gothick on the other, has two castle towers nearby. Audley's Castle is on a hillock, surrounded by woods, picturesquely overlooking Audley's Roads, by the shore of which is the other tower, perhaps the original Castleward. The mansion of the Lords de Ros, premier barons of Ireland, is Oldcourt, close to Strangford, which was burnt in 1922 during 'The Troubles' of that critical time. Strangford and Portaferry both have their towers, and likewise Kilclief, close to the entrance of the Lough on the west side. So Strangford Lough was dominated by fortifications overlooking each of the useable bays and beaches, with few exceptions, along the narrows.

Ille terrarum mihi praetor omnis Angulus ridet.
('That corner of the earth, beyond all, smiles for me'.)

It is redolent of history and romance on every hill and stream and bay and island. On the Mountain it was peaceful and lovely in every season. In spring the young green of the woods was a background for the ubiquitous thickets of glorious scented, yellow whins and the intensely blue lough, and larks were singing and lapwings mewling and tumbling in the air. In summer white wings flickered like snowflakes over the water and the cries of the terns were borne like bells on the breeze. In autumn, when the heather was dying, the lonesome call of the whaup was heard, as John Masefield remembered 'that curlew-calling time of Irish dusk.' In winter the great brown hares bounded over the frosted turf, and you could hear the wild geese and all the ducks and the innumerable, haunting voices of the waders, when the flood made over the mud flats of Quoile and beat with hushed insistence on pebbly shores.

IX

SAVAGE
COUNTRY

To live, before the First World War, at the end of the Upper Ards was like living on an island, both geographically, with the sea on so many sides, and psychologically, because of its remoteness at that time. Communications were slow and erratic, and a new dimension of unreliability had recently been introduced by the use of the early internal combustion engine in public transport.

From time beyond the memory of man there had been a ferry between Portaferry and Strangford, and I suppose it had once been a manorial perquisite of the Savage family. It was certainly the kind of thing likely to be closely controlled by local lords for military as well as commercial and financial reasons. By 1911 it had long been operated by private enterprise, a number of boatmen plying in large open sailing boats like the traditional 'skylark'. There still remained one splendid relic of days long past, but I greatly fear that it may not have survived the half-century since last I saw it. This was the 'Horseboat', used as the name suggests, for ferrying horses, but also cattle and sheep and an occasional vehicle, precariously perched upon two planks placed across her gunwales amidships. She was a great open boat, perhaps some twenty-five feet overall, very broad in the beam and with unusually low freeboard amidships, to facilitate the embarkation and debarkation of animals. This gave her a distinctive sheer, and even her exceptionally heavy timbers and the drab tarring of her carvel-built hull could not entirely disguise the gracefulness of her lines. She must have been a product of the early nineteenth, or even of the late eighteenth century, and efforts ought to have been made to preserve her.

At the time when I first remember this boat she had a great, tanned, Dutch-looking sail which gave her a picturesque appearance when it was set. It was rarely that she could make a crossing in either direction under sail alone and she had to be assisted, if not entirely propelled by oars. Even an Oxford rowing coach might have picked up a hint or two from the uninhibited helmsman's exhortations to his crew, and he did not even need a megaphone. To row a dinghy (locally called a punt) across the narrows, even with a spring tide running in full force, is not so difficult or exhausting as it might appear. What is needed is an intimate knowledge of the tides, counter-tides and eddies, and complete control of one's craft, rather than an excessive expenditure of energy.

In those days nearly all incoming bulk supplies and our potato exports were carried by sea. Two little locally-owned schooners, *Loughlong* and *Witch of the Waves* and a ketch, *Ripple*, brought in all kinds of cargo from building materials to grocery supplies. Coal however, usually came in small coasting steamers. These carried larger cargoes and could handle them more quickly, with their steam-powered derricks, than could their sailing sisters with their hand-operated 'wenches'. Oddly enough, potatoes in sacks were humped by casual dock labour to the hatches of the ship's hold. There each bag was dumped from the bearer's shoulder with a heavy crunch onto a wooden slide which took it down below. There the sacks must have been heavily trodden on by the loaders. I should doubt that any of those potatoes reached the consumers in proper condition. I can recall that one French captain promptly put a stop to this and had his cargo properly loaded by means of nets lifted and lowered by his ship's derricks. Besides the schooners and the ketch, a powerful tug, the *Jim McCausland*, whose siren's high-pitched *whoop-whoop-whoop* suggested a Redskin raid, and a diving tender, *St Anthony*, were also locally owned, by a salvage and ship-breaking firm. For many years the hulk of an old wooden full-rigged ship of theirs, stripped of her topmasts, spars and standing as well as running rigging, lay desolately at anchor in the neighbouring Ballyhenry Bay. Her lines were antique and she lent a touch of romance to the scene. Lacking ballast, she rode high and her single row of dummy gunports gave an impression, if not of one of Nelson's frigates, at least of an East Indiaman in the hey-day of John Company.

August weekends were enlivened by the arrival of anything up to a score of steam drifters, whose Scottish sabbatarian crews enjoyed two days of rest, combined with the exercises of the Kirk. During their stay the air was redolent of herring, raw and fried, and filled with the screeching of 'their ain seamaws' for which the Scots are proverbially adjured to 'keep their ain fishguts'. The cry of itinerant herring vendors was as characteristic of high summer in Portaferry as the voice of the corncrake. 'Fraish hern! Fraish hern! Sweet Ardglass and Portavogie the best!' I believe these herring, straight from the sea, sold for sixpence a dozen – in modern terms 2½p. a dozen – a 'long' dozen' of thirteen at that.

Besides seaborne commerce there were also overland lines of communication. Goods could be sent and brought in by a team of carrier's carts, drawn by mules, which made a weekly journey to and from Belfast, or perhaps just to the railway station at Newtownards. This service, known as 'Convery's Kerts', was run by Jimmy Convery, better known as 'Dublin Jack', a man 'full fat and in good point'. 'Holy God! Another stone an' Ah'd be a ton!' was said to have been his reaction on tipping the scale at nineteen stone, but he could dance a sprightly jig, light-footed as a kitten.

For those who wished to travel to Belfast in the days before the motorcar came into common use, which it did not do on any scale until after the First World War, there was a choice of two routes. One depended up *THE RELIANCE*, and that was indeed a broken reed. It was an open-topped red motor-omnibus of the earliest London type, with solid tyres, and its title

The Reliance

71

shamelessly displayed on each side in large gilt capitals. This conveyance was scheduled to make the eighteen-mile journey to or from Newtownards Station in two hours, but that was assuming that all went well, which was the case only on the rarest occasions and in the most exceptional circumstances. There were scheduled intermediate stops in Greyabbey (called Greba) and Kircubbin, at convenient hostelries, where a fair proportion of the passengers took leave, in the Dickensian coaching tradition, to refresh or anaesthetise themselves for the continuation of the journey. This, apart, from technical hitches and manifest breakdowns, made a merry mockery of a timetable calculated upon inadequate data. There were many unscheduled intermediate stops according to the requirements of passengers and the delivery of parcels, which tended to involve gossipy conversations or spirited arguments with the recipients. A serious breakdown was frankly admitted only when Charlie Palmer, the conductor extraordinary and plenipotentiary, announced that he would 'foam for a relief'. I suppose it was a relief for Charlie's feelings, but since facilities for telephoning were as yet, rare on that country road, there were doubts as to whether the relief was more than a figment of his imagination. It helped to pacify the passengers, besides affording him an excuse to slip away for a quiet smoke if the situation showed sighs of becoming too hot for him to handle.

Picture such a country roadside as John Millington Synge might have chosen for the setting of a play. On one side a field of rank swedes; on the other a dreary little pebbly beach, with deep deposit of richly malodorous seaweed and a large glacial erratic boulder, inscribed with the word *'ETERNITY'* in staring white capitals. A disgruntled heron flaps sullenly away over the steely water and some redshanks hysterically protest at the violation of their sanctuary. The globe of a great, dusky-yellow hunters' moon is rising above the low mist and there is a sharp touch of autumnal chill in the air. Beside a heap of road metal the *RELIANCE* is steaming gently, like one whose race has been run. An active figure, head and shoulders within the little bonnet seems to be wrestling with serpents or confronting a cornered wildcat. The hissing comes from a carbide bicycle-lamp, which a rustic cyclist has just lit for the benefit of the driver-mechanic. He grins broadly, delighted with the unexpected entertainment. Charlie fusses agitatedly. Will it be a case for foaming? A high-pitched masculine voice, possibly that of a Portaferry resident, usually referred to as 'Fa-

La' enquires: 'Are we going to get home the night at all, Jimmy? Can you get her fixed, Man?'

'Ah'll mebbee hev her fit in an hour Mister' says the disgusted driver, 'that's if Ah kin get this ould hookumsnivvy tae hould. Mind ye, Ah say IF!' A querulous female voice takes up the enquiry, full of apprehension. 'Hi! Charlie! Are ye there? Well, away you an' foam for a relief, unless you want us foamin' here all night.'

'Foam me Ant! Sure Jimmy'll hev her fixed anny minute. Won't ye Jimmy?'

Another shriller, uninhibited, female voice from the upper deck: 'Aye, that's right, so it is Charlie. Away you an'foam for yer Ant! Sure she'd be a sight more use'n you skittherin' about down there like un oul' goat on a skatin' rink, an' us sitting' up here like a lock⁶ of turkeys on a fence, wi' the frost splittin' the threes! A good cuddy'd be betther.'

Eventually, as more passengers add their observations and exhortations, and Charlie has become nearly desperate enough to foam, Laocoön emerges from the bonnet and applies himself to the starting handle. After frantic cranking, much backfiring and several false starts, The *RELIANCE* is once more on her perilous way with a roar. Her patrons, like Housman's infant child eaten by the grizzly bear, are unaware that they have been assimilated by the public transport system of the foreseeable future. There was much talk of a railway, which never materialised.

It is hardly surprising that my parents on the whole preferred the alternative route via Strangford and Downpatrick. Either way, in my memory, one had a very early breakfast and set out with the waning moon still shining. The other route involved, first of all, the ferry. We used to cross in a big open sloop, before the owner and his elder son were sadly drowned in a squally crossing. After that we patronised something resembling – maybe it was – a captain's gig, but with only two pairs of oars wielded by ancient mariners. The fare they asked was 'what ye plase, Sorr', which was well understood to mean at least sixpence over what one knew to be the regular amount. Soon a motorboat, called the *Defender* was introduced, which speeded things up considerably. At Strangford 'Sharvin's Cars' awaited, a small fleet of outside cars, one of which

---

⁶ *That is literally a handful.*

`Something like a Captain's Gig'

carried the morning's outward mail. Thus the Irish RM might have made one
of his eventful journeys, with Slipper driving. The drive to Downpatrick
Station, some seven or eight miles, was often enough spine-chilling in the most
literal sense, for an outside car afforded no protection from the weather.

The *RELIANCE* must have expired in some last ditch, for it was soon
replaced by an open charabanc with a hood, owned by Frank Hamilton. This
was not very noticeably an improvement on its predecessor. Then, at some stage,
Dublin Jack, with all his experience of the contrariness of mules, courageously
took on motorised transport and entered the passenger trade with a single-
decker bus, completely enclosed against the weather. I think it was called
something like *ERIN'S ISLE*. The situation was a delicate one, for it tempted
people to travel in a superior conveyance of the wrong political affiliation. This
embarrassment was removed when a worthier, Unionist rival made is
appearance under the style and title of *THE PRIDE OF ULSTER*.

For the ragamuffin element in the village, as well as for some of their elders
of equivalent mental age, the rival buses became political symbols of the highest

significance. Their old squeeze-bulb horns gave forth potent clarion-calls to party strife at this level of intelligence. Their arrival in the Square, early in the evening, was awaited with mounting excitement by crowds of juvenile partisans, chanting do-it-yourself lyrics to the tunes of the more offensive, rabble-rousing, party songs. The leading bus, whether crammed with passengers or uneconomically empty, was greeted with ecstasy by its yelling, cheering, prancing partisans, racing alongside and in front, shrilly mocking the adherents of its vanquished opponent. It was a very famous victory! I would not be surprised to learn that these auto-political contests continued until the take-over by the Transport Authority.

X

ORANGE
AND GREEN

Since we went to live in Portaferry in June, the first event I experienced
there came soon afterwards on 'The Twalft' - of July, of course! For days
beforehand men were busy erecting skeleton arches and decorating them with
flags and bunting. On the eve of the great day the finishing touches were added
with fresh flowers. I do not suppose that Sweet William, appropriate though it
might seem, was ever used. That would probably have been deemed frivolous,
and this was not a frivolous occasion. Only the Orange Lilies, sacred to the
patron king, formed the floral part of the decorations. The flags had been mass-
produced for the coronation of King George V and Queen Mary. These were
union jacks with an inset portrait of the royal pair, which, as the years rolled on,
became rain-washed pink, producing a mass effect of an oddly subdued kind,
The fife-and-drum band had, for weeks past, been working itself up in the
Orange Hall to processional pitch.

On 'The Twalft' itself we were all awakened, much to our annoyance, long
before the scraich o'day, not by the bird of dawning, but by the shuffling of
many feet and the sound of hoarse whispers and stifled laughter. The feelings of
our elderly, kindly, Catholic neighbours may be imagined, even if they saw the
funny side of the proceedings. Suddenly there was a stentorian whisper: 'There's
ould Tam in his nighshirt! Let her go, boys!' Then the musical equivalent of
spitting on the hands employed by every para-military band: Birralirralirralirra
Boomp! Birralirralirralirra Wham! And straight into 'The Protestant Boys'.
Until the sun had well risen the aubade could be heard along the shore and in
street after street, like a receding air raid.

'A weaver by trade'

I have seen a full-scale Orange procession only once in my life, but that was enough to make me feel that I have seen them every one since 1795. This one must have been in 1912 or 1913. 'The Field' on that occasion happened to be in the demesne, close by, where the Walter Meadow provided a natural amphitheatre, and the procession passed directly in front of our house. Memory has preserved only one vivid scene from the tedious march of lodge after bowler-hatted lodge, each preceded by its giant, billowing banner, borne up upon twin poles, with small boys or youths employed to hold the tasselled ropes fastened to the tops of the poles, fore and aft, to act as stays. A bearded fifer in a short tailed coat (surely Bob Williamson in person) was mopping and mowing, like King David before the Ark of the Covenant, as he played and danced in front of the monstrous Lambeg Drum, which was being waltzed like Matilda. It was obvious that he had had his beard dyed for the great occasion, presumably intending that it should flaunt one of the colours of the Order, orange or purple or true-blue. By some dire miscalculation, or by the malice of Fate, or of the barber, it had come out blazing emerald green.

The other side had their day too. I am not sure of the date, but my memory associates it with summer rather than spring. Their supporters must have included many shades of Nationalist opinion, but it was obviously very much a Catholic affair. Home Rule, it should be remembered, was not an exclusively Catholic aspiration, even in Ulster. Some distinguished Protestants were associated with the movement, while among its opponents were a few embittered enough, it was said, to have specially-made lavatory pans containing a portrait of Mr Gladstone. What collectors' pieces they would be now! With the passing of Mr Asquith's Home Rule Bill in the House of Commons in 1912, the more extremist elements on both sides were increasing their influence. Even an eight-year-old could hardly have been unaware of the atmosphere of growing tension and the feeling of crisis at the time. I can well remember the stern faces of a group of Unionists, all of whom I knew well, who went from Portaferry to a great rally near Belfast, at Balmoral, This was for the signing of the Ulster Covenant, utterly rejecting Home Rule and pledging its signatories to resist it by all means, including force.

By the time of the big Nationalist celebration that I remember taking place that Summer Sunday, tension had undoubtedly increased. It was a martyrs' memorial event. The Square, with its fine old Market House in the middle, had been the scene of a skirmish between the Yeomanry (cavalry) unit and some of the United Irishmen who had rebelled in 1798. The memory of the insurgents who fell had, ostensibly, been kept green in every sense of the word. The record of the spots where they had fallen may or may not have been handed down 'from patriot sire to patriot son'. On the Sunday of the celebration each of these sacred spots had been marked with a green-painted keg, which supported a small green banner with blood-red Gaelic lettering. The inscription on each followed exactly the same pattern: 'Here [Danny Boy or whoever it was], died for Ireland'.

In this procession the green-velour hat was as much in evidence as the bowler hat in the Orange procession. This seemed to have become the successor to the *caubeen* as a headpiece for the display of the national colour. They marched to the rhythm of sounding brass, and musically it was a celebration of Tom Moore as much as of anyone. The Minstrel Boy swaggered up to the Square, to hang his riven harp symbolically on the wall of the Market House, which the Yeomanry had held. Erin's endearing young charms were recalled emotionally along with those of Dark Rosaleen. The many supporters who had crossed over by ferry, abandoning Tom Moore as they re-embarked in the stilly night, announced loudly that they would stick to the Wearing o' the Green.

There is a bitter irony in all this. Irishmen of all persuasions have a most tenacious memory for the history of their country, if not one particularly noted for careful attention to accuracy. Protestants, especially Presbyterians, lamentably ill-informed, passed by the memorial banners, their heads turned aside and (to borrow a phrase that Burns, in Elysium, no longer needs) their gruntles twisted in a glunch of sour disdain. They ought to have known that the founder of the United Irishmen was a Dublin Protestant, Wolfe Tone, and that the Adjutant General of the insurgent forces in County Down in 1798 was the Reverend William Steel Dickson. He was one of my father's predecessors as Presbyterian minister in Portaferry. He ought to be remembered with compassion as a staunch upholder of a cause that was a Presbyterian cause in 1798, the cause of freedom. Although he was spared execution, he suffered much and died in grievous poverty. English governments from time immemorial, characteristically obtuse in all things Irish, had not merely alienated the Presbyterian section of the Planters in Ulster, whose interest might have been supposed by rational Englishmen to lie in supporting the English cause; but by imposing viciously penal religious, social and political disabilities upon them, as upon Catholics, enraged them to the point of emigration and revolt. Many Ulster Presbyterian refugees in the United States became political leaders, prominent especially in the drafting, signing and publication of the Declaration of Independence. Their descendants have provided fourteen Presidents of the United States, twenty-eight per cent of the total number. Quite a number of the insurgents who fought in Portaferry Square in 1798 were probably Presbyterians of Scottish descent.

This is only one example of the kind of political and religious mythology that has bedevilled the Irish peoples for centuries. Equally unfounded is the belief that Ulster's freedom, religion and laws were, as the slogan has it, bestowed by King William. They certainly were not, or only in the sense that he prevented King James and his ally, the French dictator, King Louis XIV, from gaining control in Ireland. Neither King James nor King William cared tuppence for any Irish cause, as such. James wanted Ireland as a base for the recovery of his English throne, which William was determined to prevent. King

Louis' object was French dominance in Europe and elsewhere, which made King William and his ally, the Pope, his sworn enemies.

In Portaferry long ago people, very sensibly, kept out of the way of each other's processions. In the main, the villagers were peaceable folk, and with a few outstandingly disagreeable exceptions on each side, there was an absence of bitterness in daily life. As time went on, there came a degree of social contact in sports like hunting, football, golf, tennis and badminton. Perhaps the common interests of a rather isolated community tended to outweigh the separatist, sectarian feelings that were so sadly prominent in larger towns and cities. When, for whatever reason, a feeling of sectarian tension was aroused, this was instantly recorded on the sensitive seismograph of the juvenile community in black looks, snarls, insults and fights. Among adults, apart from some drunken brawl, it simply meant that people, who ordinarily passed the time of day very civilly with one another, preferred not to speak. Perhaps it was the easiest way to avoid unintentionally giving offence, and I think that was understood by everyone.

XI

MASTERPIECES
AND CURIOSITIES

*T*hese two words are used, between them, to cover a wide range of subtle distinctions and characters out of the common run. At one extreme might be found the genuine scholar, the amateur of some subject, the bore of some hobby and the all-too-clever Dick, whose thought-processes eluded the man on the Glengormley bus, or even on the RELIANCE. The other extreme comprised, not, it is true, the insane afflicted by God, but the ostensible village idiot, suspected of being a good deal less deranged than might appear. There were, for example, the two small boys who were incorrigible scroungers, and indeed their need was sore. They earned what they got by a powerfully dramatic act, organised, it seemed, by the elder boy. He was overheard coaching the younger boy in these terms: '...and shake, ye bugger ye, *shake* or Ah'll gie ye a bat on the gob.' The juvenile lead threw a most realistic fit at the door of some likely prospect, and really looked as if he were just about to expire on the spot of starvation and exposure.

Portaferry did not lack colourful characters, some highly respectable, others decidedly less so, but respectability has nothing to do with the distinctions I am recalling, nor has social status, nor financial situation.

First in the procession I am assembling comes 'Rollicking' James Tomelty, a very likeable, lean, lively, little man with sparkling eyes and a captivating, if slightly rueful, smile. This was not, I think, just a courageous front exhibited to a hard world. He probably acquired his Rollicking nickname in infancy and bore it gallantly until the day he died, for his was surely happiness of the heart. Rollicking was a painter and decorator by trade and a very good one, but he had

81

other qualities and other talents. Obviously he was an agreeable companion and an amusing talker and storyteller. Above all, he had music in his blood, for he was an admirable fiddler, in the good old Irish tradition, which would have given him an honourable place in Gaelic society in earlier centuries. He was greatly in demand at concert, ceilidh and wake; I refer to the 'American Wake' for a departing emigrant, but James might have played an appropriate requiem for the passenger on the more dreaded ferry. He was a family man and his children seemed to have inherited his happy temperament. They went about their tasks and their games with a good, rousing, ra-the-ra chorus, led by the boy Joseph later the well-known Ulster actor, playwright and author.

Do the wee, little girls, I wonder, still sit on the sea wall and sing, in drawling chorus, this lullaby?

> Wan-two-three-*ah*-lee-ry
> I-spy-Miss-*Mc*-Clee-ry
> Sitt-ing-on-her-bum-*ba*-lee-ry
> Ea-ting-bre-ad-*and*-but-ter

They were well aware that a Miss McCleery was likely to be within earshot.

Robert McFadden was the proprietor of a drapery and outfitting establishment in the Square. The premises of his main competitor, the firm of Lawson, were on another side of it, in an imposing Georgian house which, at one time, underwent renovation. The proprietors caused to be printed on the façade, in ornamental lettering, the words ESTABLISHED OVER A HUNDRED YEARS. The astute McFadden, not to be upstaged with impunity, promptly placed in his unostentatious window, a notice which read ESTABLISHED YESTERDAY. NO OLD STOCK.

Eechie-Ochie, as the name so clearly indicates, was an unfortunate man with a cleft palate, to whom pithy sayings and indelicate comments were freely attributed, 'Listen to what Eechie-Ochie said' was a sure way of circulating a good story, or a dirty crack, or any piece of gossip. It was very much open to abuse by the ill-natured, who enjoyed, as a bonus, the counter-productive efforts of Eechie-Ochie to exculpate himself.

Jamie was ostensibly a simple, innocent kind of man. When electricity was first installed in the village, it was, at a shilling a unit, a very expensive luxury in those days just before the Great War. Jamie, in his simple, innocent way, simply ran a line from the nearest pole to his residence. He was too innocent to know about switches, or perhaps his source of supply did not run to such refinements. The consequent shining of his light before men soon revealed his good works. Presented with a summons, he seized an axe, threatened the policeman and tried to fell the pole from which his trap-line led. It was believed that charges arising from this episode afforded some consolation to the officer, who had failed to establish an earlier charge of illicit distilling.

Mr Rogers, Manager of the Belfast Bank (then in the seafront house now occupied by the Queen's University Marine Biology Department) was a most impressive paterfamilias. He affected muttonchop whiskers, a sweeping moustachio and a stock ornamented with a Connemara marble shamrock stick-pin, the whole underwritten, as it were, by a nicely rounded undercarriage. Suave in manner with adults, he was splendidly irascible with small boys and dogs. He delighted irreverent youth, not by the unquestionable dignity of his

'Parliament of Men'

83

port, but by bathing daily in the nude, prancing in feet foremost from a flexible springboard with a stupendous splash.

Cream-to-the-Bottom was a milk roundsman. He was uncommonly accident-prone and one felt that a wicked fairy had officiated as godmother and that malign influences combined against him. While learning to drive (a much more difficult thing then than it is now) he had the misfortune to back into his sworn enemy, the sergeant of police. The officer promptly charged him with a number of offences, informing the bench that Cream-to-the-Bottom had said, compounding the offences, 'It was all your own fault. Sure you're always in the road anyway!' That was a point of view to which many would have subscribed.

Willie, the Church of Ireland Sexton, was a very fierce Orangeman. He played the bass drum in the band, offhandedly maintaining a precarious rhythm with a single drumstick in the left hand. His right arm rested upon the cylinder of the drum and he leant nonchalantly upon it as he marched. Willie was fond of a noggin, and, easily aroused, he freely gave tongue to his thoughts. Some youths, bullocking about on the steps of the church before a harvest festival, were cordially invited: 'Will yez, for God's sake, come in tae Hell, ot get out tae blazes!' Any delicate or elderly person, who incurred the Sexton's displeasure, was told contemptuously that 'sure Ah'll sune be givin' ye a shlap on the beak wi' a spade!' Aggressive though he could be, there was said to be one sure way of cutting him down to size. The historic episode in his career occurred when, a good deal under the influence of his potations, he attended an auction. Maybe the keen auctioneer, who once inadvertently - or perhaps not - sold his own hat, seeing Willie's interest in a picture, encouraged him to bid. After some spirited counter-bidding, Willie eventually acquired what he believed to be a portrait of King William 'of glorious, pious and immortal memory'. Ever after, almost any remark of the Sexton's was apt to be capped with 'aye, Willie, I suppose that was the day you bought the Pope!'

Another Willie was a blacksmith, one of three brothers, each on his own in the same trade, and fully employed before the farm horse gave way to the tractor, which, when not working, did not eat. He was a tall man, thin and hollow-cheeked, deep chested and with long, sinewy arms. He wore a very ancient pair of steel-framed spectacles, with small oval lenses of a kind common in the time of Mr Pickwick, through which he peered short-sightedly. His voice was harsh and apt to shift into a higher register in moments of surprise or indignation. His talk was tedious, but he could be interesting about 'th'ould days', if you had the patience to listen. Like so many of his craft, he was also a horse-doctor and always ready to lay down the law in all matters equine. Here is his opinion about a therapeutic dose for a horse, which I have from a discourse of his noted down by my father by 1914.

'Now aconite —ye've heerd av aconite? Aconite's the thing for th' inflammation, an' many's the row ould Mr Medonn'l an' me had about th'aconite. He w'uld only allow five dhraps – five dhraps, ye know, is a dose f'r a hoarse. Five dhraps, n'yaye, he w'uld only allow five dhraps, but in some cases it's not enough. No! An' Ah hev give up till ten dhraps, and' Ah'll hould ye f'r a ha'penny that 'uld warm his arse f'r 'm! Ah b'lieve while there's life there's hope an' Ah power it in till it goes wan way or th'other. Yis, wan way or th'other.' A little of Willie went a long way.

It would be misleading to present Billy as a typical representative of the local fishermen. He was undeniably a fisherman and a very skilful one, but he was essentially something more and that something was of great importance in his trade. His conversation did much to promote the sale of his fish and even more to promote remuneration commensurate with his entertainment value, fish or no. There he stands – again thanks to my father – on our doorstep in his utterly disreputable garments, a small string of evenly-matched fish dangling from a finger. Beneath the peak of his seaman's cap a great rosy nose (for he claimed to have drunk, in his time, enough to float the Ryal Jarge, or buy a funnel for her anyway) is flanked by small, cunning dancing, devil-may-care eyes. His bronzed, wrinkled face is framed in a frill of unkempt, grey whiskers and a goatee beard. Above one ear

'Billy'

the red heads of several matches can be seen amid the elf-locks. He is merry and unconcerned, quick and never at a loss for a retort. Bessie has gone to the door, for business is to be done between high contracting parties and not through any menial intermediary. There is a powerful aroma of Old Bushmills or John Jameson. Billy has brought precisely the number and size of fish that he knows will be required, for even if there are guests he will know about their presence. He might have been observed, a few minutes earlier, taking similar appropriate strings of fish to neighbouring houses from a large box in his boat.

'There's me night's fishin, m'em,' says he with melancholy resignation.

'You haven't had much luck then, Billy?'

'Luck! Ah wus out at the mouth av the river, an' as sure as Ah'm tellin ye, they jist et me bait an'tuk it wi' them, an' wan big feila tuk heuk an' all, an' if ye call sittin' at the Pladdy Lug feedin' the fishes luck, then Ah hed luck an' plenty av it. Naw, there was nathin' doin'.'

'Well, I hope you have better luck next time. Tell me, Billy, what do you thing the weather is going to do?'

'The weather? Well now, Ah'm blowed, but see here, ye hev me bate. Ah'm no prophet, nor me father afore me, but the wun's in the s'uth'ard and' ye kin hev no guid weather outa Kileef – ye've heerd av dirty Kileef? But if the wun shifts tae westh'ard an' then shifts roun' tae the nor'ard, when it blows a while over the Walther Meada, ye'll hev the fine weather. If it gets a ketch, it'll hould'.

'Well, you ought to nail it Billy, when it does get round'.

'Well, so Ah sh'uld an' Ah hev the nail that'll hould it, if ye can just get me the hammer that'll dhrive it!'

'Billy, you're terribly wet. It's well you've had a good jorum.'

'Sure Ah jist take it nate, ye know, an lave the weather tae wather it.'

'But even neat it will not keep you from getting your death of cold. You had better hurry home and get your clothes dried.'

'Och, bedad! They'll jist hev tae dhry on the same bush they got wet on. Well, guid day t'ye, m'em, an' Ah wish ye health and more prosperity.'

The sting in that leave-taking lay in the penultimate word. I suppose my mother, who thought Billy just an old reprobate, had not paid him as much extra as he considered his due.

Once a conversation touching upon schools elicited this saga.

'Sure Ah was a monithor in the Methody Bailey's School. Sometimes he w'uld lave me in charge, an' when Ah shtruck the dask wi' the cane an' shouted 'Silence!' be Jiminy! Ye'd a heerd thim over the wather there in the village beyant!' Billy, when prompted, went on to explain why he had not persevered in the scholastic profession.

'Well, it wus this way: Ah wus takin' the Jographi class, an' Ah hed tae gie wan o' thim a bat on the jaw f'r his igerance an' imperence. So th'ould Methody, he called me up an' says he tae me 'Willum, tha's no way til tache Jographi' he says. 'Now', says he, put yer head underneath the table', an' be the Tarnal Post, whin he hed me down he give we wan blatther that made me lep like a goat, an' Ah tuk intil the dasks with him aftiter me till Ah got the dhoor open, an Ah left.'

By this time the story was going so well that Billy had begun to believe it himself, so he went on to explain that this experience had not put an end to his formal education. Undaunted, he went to another establishment 'where all the gintry av Portaferry went'. 'But ould Tammy wus a terror. Sure he hed thim all black an' blue, He wanted tae bate me wan day an' Ah w'uldn't let him. Ah jist tould him 'Ah'll put that slate intil ye', Ah says. At that he tuk wan runnin' race at me an' Ah flung the slate. Sowl! If thon slate hed 'a hut him on the head, ould Tam's number would have been up! So Ah opened the dhoor an' left, an' aftiter that Ah wen taa seã.'

Billy had a vivid, if limited, imagination. He swore by strange gods, some unprintable, some mysterious like the Tarnal Post, some romantic, like the Light 'at Shines. It was Mr Filson Young who stencilled one of the printable kind, *Holy Fly*, on the transom of Billy's old boat, which proudly bore this distinguished editorial impress until her master's demise in the fullness of years.

XII

SOUND,
SOUND THE CLARION

*I*ndeed. And fill the fife too! Children are acutely conscious, at a surprisingly early age, of the social conventions and attitudes of grownups, while much else may escape them in which they are not greatly interested. I am quite clear that, by the summer of 1912, when I was rising eight, political events and the attitude of grownups to them were making a very definite impact upon me. The reason, I suppose, was that they showed signs of affecting me personally. It is difficult, at the distance of these years, to recall sequences of events and reactions in the order in which they occurred. What I am about to write may be taken as applying to a period of about two years, or a little more, before the outbreak of the First World War.

It seems ironical that the political heirs of the signatories of the Ulster Covenant of 1912 should now be in the position of protesting against the suspension of Home Rule in the six-county rump of the Old Province of Ulster. Of course it was a different kind of Home Rule, for the whole of Ireland, in 1912. Perhaps the illogicality of the situation is more apparent than real, for the same things are at stake now that were at issue then, and the same fears are entertained. Mr Asquith's Home Rule Bill, passed by the House of Commons in 1912, was not (at least in the eyes of an historian) at all an unreasonable one. Protestants feared then that it would have the effect of reducing them to the status of a severely oppressed minority, and that is what they still fear in any union with the Republic. One thing is very clear to an historian: the failure to implement the Act in 1914, because of the outbreak of the First World War, discredited the moderate Nationalists and left the way open for the militants to seize control of the movement, as they did in the Easter rising of 1916.

In 1912 men returned home from signing the Covenant in a very serious frame of mind. That was not at all surprising, in view of what they had pledged themselves to do, in terms of 'No Surrender' and resistance by force. Then too, passive resisters were discredited and militants took over. It was said that some Zealots signed in their own blood. Fred gave a characteristically comic and dramatic account of the antics of one, who could not get his lifeblood to flow in the pen. Things seemed to me to be shaping rather on the lines of the early instalments of 'Sinclair of the Scouts' a West African epic that I was reading in the bound volume of *The Boys' Own Paper* for 1911. I began to hear from my Sloane cousins of the doings of their father, Jim, in the Unionist tradition of that family.

I think the greatest impact of events upon me may have resulted from a visit to my grandmother at this time of deepening crisis. I discovered that her larder, ordinarily a very well stocked one and of great interest to me, had been provisioned literally for a siege. There was an enormous barrel, and I am sure it was a barrel, of flour, sacks of oatmeal and sugar, hams and sides of bacon, huge cubical tins of tea and goodness knows what else. My grandmother's family was certainly not going to starve in an emergency, if her foresight could prevent it. She spoke to me in a matter-of-fact way, as no-one had spoken to me before, about the probability of civil war. She did not lack courage, and I think that, as a result of her forthright talk, I found the situation more exciting than terrifying. My grandmama, I confidently believed, would 'see this thing through', a phrase constantly on peoples' lips then.

The impression of impending action was strengthened in other ways. Already, before the historic gun-running, my friends and I became aware of interesting happenings in an unfrequented, but not distant, part of the demesne. Careful reconnaissance, in the best Red Indian tradition, revealed a newly constructed rifle range, obviously much in use, judging from the quantity of spent and flattened bullets at the target end. I would suspect, retrospectively, that sporting rifles, such as Winchesters, were being used. About that time I noticed some little books that I had not previously seen in the house. Thinking that they were probably hymn-books, I was not interested, but sooner or later curiosity prompted me to examine them. They turned out to be manuals of first aid and nursing. I also came across what I took to be a fishing reel of unusual size and construction, and had visions of fish far beyond the common run. It was soon revealed that this gadget had nothing to do with angling, but was designed for rolling bandages, an operation in which I was encouraged to take part, soon far beyond my wayward inclination. My mother, with her Unionist ancestry and zest for organisation, was up to something. When she appeared one afternoon in the dress of a nursing sister, it was very clear to me that the profession of Florence Nightingale (who died only in 1910) was about to receive a fundamental stimulus in Portaferry.

My mother and Dr MacDonald were forming a nursing unit to function when hostilities should break out. It eventually became a wartime Voluntary Aid Detachment. The headquarters was in the stable block of Portaferry House.

'For God and Ulster'

I soon found myself and some friends enlisted as objects upon which the aspiring nurses might practise the art, or craft, of bandaging. This proved excessively trying for all concerned, although the most notoriously mischievous of the gang had been excluded, and our services were soon dispensed with. The nurses were not, however, deprived of opportunities to practise their arts, for there was always Jeremiah. Of origin unknown to me, he was a very fine, articulated figure of a soldier, complete in every detail. He caused a deal of tittering long before Bruce Bairnsfather's famous character, Old Bill, whom he closely resembled, emerged from the 'Better 'Ole'.

Tension increased as time wore on towards the anticipated implementation of Home Rule, which could be the signal for rebellion. An event which seemed to me exciting, as well as very interesting, was obviously regarded by my elders with a good deal of apprehension. I had seen warships before, and had even been taken on a conducted inspection of HMS *Bellerophon* when the summer cruise squadron was lying in Bangor Bay, but I had never seen anything like this new event. A rakish-looking destroyer steamed into the Lough at high speed, cutting a spectacular bow wave and making light of our racing tide. After lying about for some time, she departed as swiftly as she had come, to return at frequent, irregular intervals. I wondered why, but no explanation was forthcoming, only vague speculation. Billy, when consulted, spat and made disparaging remarks about the

Bessie, 1919,
Commandant,
Portaferry Unit, VAD.

Royal Navy and all its works. The Harbourmaster, who was pretty certainly up to his neck in the illicit business, thought they must be looking for something! They were indeed, but Naval Intelligence had picked the wrong Lough. It was in Larne Lough, at Larne, and in Belfast Lough, at Bangor, that the gun-running took place.

I have no idea of the terms in which the impending civil war was regarded by all those concerned, or what lessons, if any, had been drawn from all the little frontier wars and from the recent Boer War. It would be easy, with all the grim hindsight acquired since those innocent days, to pour scorn upon the unsophisticated zealots of those years. Many of them were soon to experience war on an unparalleled scale. From that rebellious Ulster Volunteer Force there was created the Ulster Division that suffered slaughter and disaster on the first day of the battle of the Somme, 1st July, 1916.

Whatever stresses the adults on both sides suffered during the Home Rule crisis, it may fairly be said that these (to use a vulgarism of the time) 'never fizzed on' their children. My own memory is of an ordinary, playful small boy's life, especially in boats; and carefree, except for Latin.

XIII

THE EVE OF
WORLD WAR ONE

*T*he Strangford Lough Regatta week in 1914 was held at the end of July
and beginning of August. In addition to local yachts and the usual small
collection of visiting strangers, an exceptionally large contingent of all classes
from the Royal Ulster Yacht Club, including Fred and friends in *Talisman*,
assembled that year. So numerous were the yachtsmen that, on that unique
occasion, a camp was pitched for them on military lines – or was there a real
military purpose? The large assembly of yachts, perhaps the largest fleet of sail
collected there since Viking times, lay at anchor in Audley's Roads. Lines of
bell-tents were pitched on the greensward between Audley's ancient castle and
the woods, with a large marquee as a mess tent. At night they shone like glow-
worms, mingling their reflections with those of the yachts' riding lights in the
calm waters of the roadstead. Sounds of mirth and song were heard nightly,
until the small hours. Never was such lightheartedness and merriment at
regatta time. People went promenading, or drifting in boats to sing,
antiphonally with the yachtsmen, songs of Erin and popular music-hall ditties
that were so soon to give place to, 'Tipperary', 'Old Kit Bag' and 'Mademoiselle
from Armenteers'.

Portaferry regatta on Wednesday, 30th July began on a subdued note, as far
as spectators were concerned. Yachts were arriving to lie at anchor if they were
not in an early race, or to hold on and off well clear of the starting line if they
were. The crews, in white ducks, navy-blue jerseys and scarlet 'jellybag' caps,
skippers in white-topped yachting caps, made final preparations. The mark-

boat, which was the Horseboat, gay with unaccustomed bunting, was made fast to the buoy off the quay. Longshoremen and small boys watched the proceedings critically, with knowing eyes, and fairground men, the legitimate operators, that is, began to set up their stalls. There were, as always, several stalls devoted to the sale of 'yellowman', a formidable species of confectionery which, like other geological specimens, was broken by sharp hammer-blows. This was, beyond question, the ultimate in gobstoppers. Any juvenile or adult who got his teeth into it was unlikely to get his jaws apart for a good half-hour. Legitimate business was also done by shooting galleries where the deviation of the airguns was beyond calculation. Hoop-la too was within the bounds of respectability. The operator of a diminutive, hand-cranked roundabout optimistically set up his contraption for the toddlers. Other operators would make a furtive appearance when the crowd grew dense enough to afford them cover from the police, and means of escape if need be.

Soon the five-minute and starting guns were banging away, and the yachts and craft of other classes were off on the flood tide, 'beyond the bourne of time and place' for several hours. Tennyson, it was alleged, composed 'Crossing the Bar' here. Then our party embarked in a motor boat to follow the fortunes of our sailing friends. There was a fresh northerly breeze aslant the flood tide, which confused strangers to the Lough and gave natives an advantage. Many scathing comments were made about the seamanship of one, Charlie, in a big, chocolate-coloured yawl, so he was referred to as 'The Chocolate Sailor'. Perhaps he was unfamiliar with the yawl rig, for he pursued a highly idiosyncratic course, punctuated by complex Chinese gybes.

By the time we had returned home and lunched, the leading yachts were beginning to cross the finishing line. The crowd was dense by this time and the spectator events could begin. First the sailing dinghies (Strangford Lough Punts they were called) with their centreboards and towering gunter lugs were sailed with magnificent panache and perfect mastery of tidal conditions, rounding the marks like electrified Nureyevs in the now strongly running ebb. Then came various rowing events, including one for the long, slender, six-oared gigs that now seem to have vanished from the longshore scene. Finally and hilariously, the Shovel Race. This was for open boats propelled by crews wielding big, square-bladed, iron coal-shovels. The general effect was of South Seas war canoes. The courses pursued by the competing crews were undisciplined and wildly erratic, since the Guinness-inspired paddlers on one side of a boat, regardless of all the requirements of team-work, sometimes paddled, hell-for-leather, against those on the other side of their own boat, quite oblivious of rival boats. Collisions were not infrequent, giving rise, not to official protests, but to sea-fights in the Viking tradition. When a paddler accidentally splashed a fellow toiler in his own boat, eloquent flights of vituperation ensued, and both dropped their shovels, inboard or out, to come to fisticuffs. The winning boat, if winner there were, crossed the line in a slother of foam and a cloud of blasphemy, to the delighted cheers and uninhibited comments of a section of the spectators. This unedifying gladiatorial spectacle was abandoned in future years in favour of a swimming race, to the disappointment of small boys of all ages.

By now the less respectable fairground operators, with their small, collapsible tables, were doing good business. The three-card men and the thimble-riggers, with wary eyes on the movements of the constabulary, were happily fleecing the bumpkins. Roulette seemed to be plied with scant regard for the minions of the Law, and a Cockney crown-and-anchor man was conducting his popular and remunerative trade in a hearty voice. 'Step up, me lads! Step up! Yer backs yer fancy and Oi pyes yer prompt. Hup she comes an'

In the Viking tradition

wot 'ave we got? Two mud-'ooks and' one sar'nt mijor. 'Ard line me lad. Better luck next tahm! 'Ave another go?'

Later in the afternoon the crowd moved into the Walter Meadow to witness a football match against Slanes, then Portaferry's keenest rival. This was followed by sports, some of which have not yet been recognised for Olympic honours. Several mendicants were aggressively in action, for this was their big day. Prominent among them was a very pertinacious mariner, victim of a fire at sea, who made inarticulate but menacing noises, while exhibiting his revolting scars and mutilated limbs and torso. There was no Welfare State to care for him.

The big events remained to be contested at the end of the meeting, and they attracted by far the greatest interest and enthusiasm. This is where the Olympic authorities have fallen down so badly. The contests were the Greasy Pig and the Greasy Pole. A terrified young porker, thickly coated with soft soap, having been released, the competitors, few of them entirely sober, staggered in vociferous pursuit. Some of the hand-offs would have done credit to a Welsh rugby three-quarter heading for a runaway try. The crowd roared. Inevitably the pig got among the legs of the spectators, with much human as well as porcine squealing. The ensuing recriminations were very promptly suppressed by the police, under whose supervision the competitors drew lots for the pig. This was doubtless a scandalously illegal proceeding, but an eminently practical way of dealing with a situation that might so easily have caused trouble.

There remained the climactic Greasy Pole. At the truck of this mast there hung a large ham; a little lower down a pair of boots dangled, and, lowest of all, a pair of thick grey socks. Several competitors arrived on the scene specially equipped for the ascent. One had a paper bag full of fine ash to coat the palms of his hands and the insides of his arms and legs. Another, in addition to being well primed with porter, carried a length of elaborately knotted line. He stepped into the arena, proclaiming in a loud voice that 'thon ould ham' was his and that the contest was a meaningless formality. Competitor after competitor failed and slid ignominiously to earth, and so the grease was partly wiped off the pole, but it still remained sufficiently slippery. At last one lad succeeded in snatching the socks amid applause and ribaldry. Then a great, tow-headed mooncalf just managed to unhitch the boots before plummeting to the ground on his fat behind, with them falling round his ears. There was a pause. Anyone for the ham? The knotted-line contestant made an inelegant locution to the effect that he would now, without further delay, remove the ham that was rightfully his. It seemed that, as at a similar juncture in *Ivanhoe*, no other challenger would be forthcoming to contest the issue. But 'a single trumpet breathed defiance'. A small, thin, shock-headed boy was suddenly unleashed by his handler, at what he rightly conceived to be the moment of truth. This infant, before anyone quite realised what was happening, soared by some mysterious means of levitation to the top of the pole, detached the ham, descended triumphantly and disappeared into the crowd. His departure was accompanied by plangent, crudely-framed complaints of foul play from the gunked champion.

Now it was time for the presentation of the trophies and prizes, while hucksters and tricksters continued their activities by the light of napha flares, which shed a lurid light on the scene. The crowd surged round the tall flight of steps leading to the old Bank House. Such an occasion could not be allowed to pass without floods of oratory, punctuated by the comments of the audience and cries of the fairground men. The orator eulogised the organizers of the Regatta, collectively and individually, extolled the efforts of the great concourse of yachtsmen, including the Chocolate Sailor [*Gybe, ye dog ye! Gybe!*] praising the munificence of the generous donors of [*An' wot'ave we got?*] the handsome silver rose bowl, the cups and other valuable prizes which had been competed for in the best tradition of Irish sportsmanship. [*Hurrah! Hi Paddy! Who fell off the powl? Who ate the poultice aff the chile's head? Me han' on yer rope, Paddy!*] Now, if Dr McLaughlin, third time winner of the Handicap Race in his famous old cutter *Seahorse*, that has been winning prizes in Strangford Lough since [*Brian Boru! Up Dochtor! Up the ould Salt Horse! Up! Up! Up! ...an' one mud'ook*] so through the long list of prizes, including £2 for *Annalong*, winner of the fastest shovel race ever seen here and her splendid crew, Bill Bailey, Jimmy Daly, Danny Lyon, Paddy Ryan, Mick Nolan, Sam Rolan, Wee Willie McGorrian and all, who crossed the finishing line like the *RELIANCE* herself [*Who towed her in?*] in the fastest time ever recorded in Portaferry Regatta [*Will yez for Jasus' sake, bhoys, c'mon tae McGraws before they're shut. Yer last chance ... an' THREE sar'nt mijors. There's your luck!*] So ended Portaferry Regatta on Wednesday, 30th July. Other regattas occupied the next three days.

On Saturday night the yachtsman in camp celebrated with a grand firework display. I went to sleep with the sounds of singing, cheering and bursting rockets in my ears.

When I looked out that Sunday morning, only two forlorn yachts remained at anchor in Audley's Roads. I had read the newspaper headlines and had heard my father speak with deep concern and indignation about the Kaiser's view of the treaty guaranteeing the neutrality of Belgium as a 'scrap of paper'. I was intelligent enough to understand that war was likely to result, although I had not the faintest conception of what the reality of war would be. All this I had forgotten, as so many grown-ups had forgotten it, in the excitement of Regatta time. Indeed the attitude of the general public at this stage was one of jaunty optimism, rather as though a military tattoo, rather than a war, was about to be staged.

On that Sunday morning my mother told me that Fred had come over, late the previous night, to say that he and his friends had been called to the colours and were off at once to join their Territorial unit. All the other yachtsmen too, with that single purpose, had quietly slipped out to sea. The desolate scene seemed to me like the end of the world. The outbreak of the Great War on 4th August 1914 did indeed mark the end of the world I had known during the first decade of my life. It could never be the same again.

APPENDIX

Reply to the moderator's request for prayer prior to the election, January, 1910

Right Reverend Sir, I have your note
Requesting prayer about the vote,
That, mid the strife and din of faction,
The Lord should guide the next election,
But you, forsooth, forgot to say
What party ought to win the day,
Unless, by what the leaders be,
You state it inferentially.

What is a common man to do,
Who tariff wants and budget too,
That, lost in wonder, all behold
Our taxes paid in foreign gold,
And that the straining mule may know
Its crushing burden lighter grow,
When portion of its load compass
The shoulders of the Lordly ass?

But surely you must know, I ween
That party politics isn't clean;
That he who to a place aspires
Must know the art of pulling wires,
And, if the Commons would adorn,
Must give rich largesse, night and morn,
Besides, some leaders set the pace
And clearly want to win their case.

So to invoke the Lord's assistance
Would seem like bouncing all resistance,
For surely Providence would not care
To be a Little Englander,
And did He enter to the lists
Would be among the Unionists.

I'm neither Croppy, Whig nor Tory
And seek no Parliamentary glory,
And do not care a single fluke
For any viscount, lord or duke,
But when the Church grows enterprising
I cannot keep my gorge from rising,
When nine or ten ex-Moderators
Assume the role of gladiators.

Now, John O'Prayer, don't think me drastic,
But there's John the great scholastic,
And for a coming Moderator,
There's Mission John, a dacent crathur.
See how they strain with lathered side,
With flaming eye and nostril wide,
Dragging, with many a bump and lurch,
The straining chariot of the Church.

There, mounted on the perch behind,
The Editor of the Blast of Wind,
And you, while lurching here and there,
Grasp at the sides and call for prayer.

Now, if you'd take advice from me,
You'd drive the chariot leisurely
By gently putting on the brake;

Then these Aposites firmly take,
Snaffle and bit each silken nose,
Shake out the reins, and there - Repose!

What shall we ask the Lord to do?
Turn on the spigot, or the screw?
Ask him to clean the daily papers
By substituting truth for vapours?
Or shall we take another line
And say, with easy unctious whine,

Lord, we remember well this day
The Belfast University,
And we are also grieved to see
The parlous state of poor Magee.
Now look on supple-minded Birrell,
The laughing jay and chattering squirrel,
Who made us, when his plans uncurled,
The laughing stock of half the world
Lay bare thy gret right arm and make
This creature in his breeches shake,
Give him a most tremendous licking
And, when that's done, we'll do the kicking.
Of knighthoods we require a few
To pay Church debts, long overdue,
So, in thy mercy, spare the Lords,
Strengthen our stakes, prolong our cords,
And if the poor have been too frisky
On patent or on pot-still whiskey,
The poor are thriftless, casual doers.
Restrain the Trade, but spare the brewers?
But there, I'll stop. It's very clear
That things are very mixed, John dear!
It matters not how pure you plea,

'Tis useless, Sir, as you can see,
To set, with so much anxious bother,
The one side praying 'gainst the other.
They'll pray, but to the ballot go
And vote for Party, Lord or no!
I am, in haste to catch the mail,
Yours very truly, Jamie Flail.

JAMES KENNEDY CRONNE

I have this text only in the original,
scribbled draft, obviously Jimmy did not
think much of it and never bothered to polish it up.
I have taken the liberty of breaking up, somewhat arbitrarily,
the continuous whole.

INDEX

Place and personal names

Portaferry from the Quay

O litel book, thou art so unconning,
How darst thou put thy-self in prees for dreds

CHAUCER